1

The Must See Hiking Destinations of Long Island

An all encompassing guide to Long Island and its Pine Barrens

James Daniels

ISBN:9781947962019
email --jdhiking@optimum.net

Library of Congress Control Number: 2017915503

Picture on front cover- from the top of the Fire Island
Lighthouse in Fire Island National Seashore

To the best of my knowledge, all the information
presented in this book is accurate. However, things
change so check with the proper authorities before your
hike, and remember, hiking has its hazards so prepare
properly.

To my dog, Candee, for accompanying us on almost all

of our hikes, leading the way to solitude

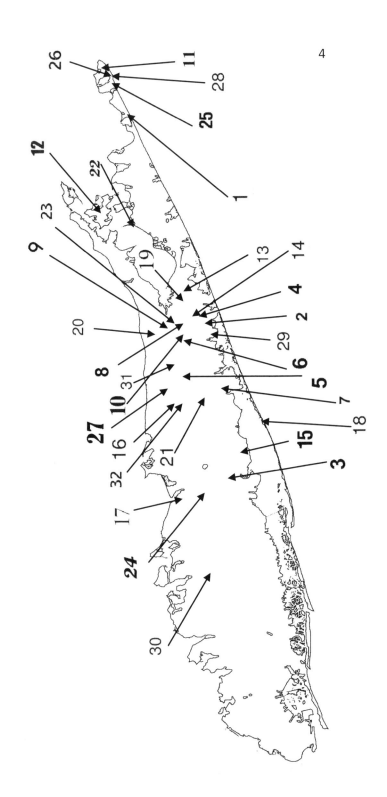

4

Contents

Introduction

The first thing you might do when you pick this up is say "Hiking on Long Island? Really?". Most people don't know it but Long Island has many great hikes scattered throughout the area. There are a plethora of preserves and state parks to be found along with the highest concentration of county parks in the entire state. In the Pine Barrens Core Preservation Area alone there is 55,000 acres of undeveloped land. Plus there are many other unique parks outside of that area that are worth exploring such as Hither Hills State Park and Wildwood State Park. Long Island is a great place because you can escape the hustle and bustle and get hiking in a matter of minutes.

The Pine Barrens

Our island has a wilderness called the Pine Barrens. The Pine Barrens is what most of the land on Long Island was protected for because it harbors many rare species and helps cleanse our drinking water. When you are driving you might notice what are called recharge basins with a fence surrounding them. They are meant to help collect rainwater and filter it through the ground which the Pine Barrens does for us naturally. Almost all of our drinking water comes from the aquifers and the Pine Barrens are crucial in keeping it clean. The porous, sandy soil works to help take out pollutants from the water when it passes through it.

Eventually, it reaches one of the three main aquifers which are the Upper Glacial Aquifer, the Lloyd Aquifer, and the Magothy Aquifer. The Magothy Aquifer is the biggest but the Lloyd is the furthest underground. The Lloyd Aquifer is 1,800 feet below the surface and the water is 6,000 years old which is about the time of the invention of writing. New York regulates the amount of water that can be pumped from it to ensure that it is around for future generations to come.

Back in the 1700s, most of the trees in northern Suffolk County were cut down for firewood and building material. The choice tree to chop down would have been a deciduous tree not a pitch pine due to a pitch pine's little commercial value. This left most of the pines in Suffolk County untouched which actually contributed to the expansion of the Pine Barrens. So by the late 1700s, what once was mostly a deciduous forest in Suffolk County turned into classic Pine Barrens you see today. In 1790 George Washington described an area from Patchogue to Coram as "low scrubby oak, ... intermixed with small and ill-thriven pines". The Pine Barrens in this time period stretched all the way from Nassau County to the Twin Forks. It's amazing to think that human interference caused the growth of the Pine Barrens several hundred years ago but also caused the Pine Barrens to shrink in the 1900s due to housing developments. The Pine Barrens today is comprised of the Core Preservation Area and the Compatible Growth Area which total over 100,000 acres but at its peak the Pine Barrens were around 247,000 acres.

What else you may not know is that there are several types are carnivorous plants on Long Island such as the sundew or pitcher plant. There is also an endangered buck moth that lives in the sandy soil of the dwarf pines that comes out for a beautiful sight in October. The Pine Barrens are truly amazing because they encompass so many great natural features such as rare coastal plains ponds, the dwarf pines, marshes, kettle holes, 100 foot white pines, and much more. Hike number six will take you out of the suburbs and into a wonderful hike that passes coastal plains ponds. These ponds, which you will learn more about, are very unique harboring many rare species and much more. The dwarf pines, which you will read about in hike two, are found in only three places in the entire world. They rarely grow above 20 feet in the poor, sandy soil of Westhampton. Since we live on an island the land eventually meets the ocean so here we find saltwater marshes at for example Wertheim National Wildlife Refuge (hike seven). In Prosser Pines County Park you walk through a mini redwood forest of white pine trees planted in 1812 by Mr. Dayton. These trees are magnificent and make for a great, short hike for people of all ages.

Lastly, there are two major rivers in the Pine Barrens. One of them is the Carmen's River which goes through Wertheim National Wildlife Refuge and Southaven County Park. The other is the Peconic River that starts at the Peconic Bay and goes all the way to the Brookhaven Lab. These two rivers are excellent spots for canoeing and kayaking.

Our Glacial History

Since our island was formed by the Wisconsin Glacier many thousands of years ago it left behind traces of its past. One of these traces is called glacial erratics which are essentially big boulders left behind when the glaciers melted. Many of these erratics are found in Manorville Hills County Park (hike ten). In Manorville Hills you can see the largest concentration of inland glacial erratics on Long Island. It is called the Boulder Field and can be accessed by the Paumanok Path. Some of the erratics on Long Island can be larger than a person. However, the biggest erratic on Long Island weighs 5 million pounds and is 55 feet by 35 feet. It is called Shelter Rock and was used by the Indians as a shelter, hence its name. Another example of our glacial past is kettle holes that were formed when the glaciers retreated and left basically a big depression in the ground. On Long Island they don't get too big but in Canada they could be over 400 acres which is quite large. The kettle holes on our island are basically a depression which sometimes turn into vernal ponds. There is a pretty big one next to Suffolk Community College in Riverhead along a trail that connects to the Paumanok Path. The last thing our glaciers did was form moraines which are an accumulation of solids left by a glacier. One of the moraines on Long Island is the

Ronkonkoma Moraine which runs across most of the island. It reaches its peak in the Manorville Hills area where the hills are about 300 feet tall in some spots. It doesn't seem like a lot but you can see for miles at the top of some of the hills providing excellent views of the surroundings. One of these hills is called Bald Hill, located in Riverhead, which has an elevation of 295 feet (hike 8). Atop this hill you can see for miles to the north and east affording great views of the town of Riverhead. The tallest hill on the island, however, is Jane's Hill with an elevation of 400 feet above sea level. This is covered in hike 26 at West Hills County Park on the western end of Long Island. Jane's Hill is part of the Harbor Hill Moraine which is farther north than the Ronkonkoma Moraine. When the glaciers were melting and receding, the finer, smoother material ran off to the south forming the very sandy beaches unlike the rocky beaches of the north shore. This is called an outwash plain which is present along the south shore.

The Trees

So let's get to the composition of our forests. Most of the Pine Barrens is composed of pitch pine (on the next page) and oak which make up almost all of the canopy cover. Therefore we are called a pine-oak forest that is typical along the east coast. But unlike the other forests of the east coast, the Pine Barrens of Long Island, New Jersey, and Cape Cod are much more special. Pitch pine is a type of pine tree that likes sandy and low nutrient soil. Their needles are found in bundles of three compared to white pines which are in bundles of two. What makes a pitch pine so unique is that its trunk has plates of bark stuck together unlike a white pine's which is very smooth. These plates of bark help the pitch pine resist the heat of a wildfire making them a very resilient tree. If you go to the 2012 burn scars in Manorville you will see all of the oaks are dead

but some pitch pines survived due to their rigid outer bark. Even if almost all of the green of the tree is burnt off it can still come back. The pines repopulate using fire too and some of the pine cones will open up only during the intense heat of a forest fire. These pine cones are called serotinus. In 1995, there was the Sunrise Fire which burnt most of the Westhampton area. After the fire was over nothing was left standing, but in 20 years the seedlings took hold and sprouted a new, healthy forest. Since we live in a densely populated area, fire has been suppressed, putting the long term health of the Pine Barrens in jeopardy.

The total lifespan of a pitch pine is 200 years

and they grow about one foot per year under optimal growth compared to the white pine which can grow up to four feet per year. Pitch pine is most predominant in the Pine Barrens since white pine is only found in about four groves in Suffolk County. Scrub oak is another important part of the Pine Barrens because it requires a lot of sunlight making it well adapted for fire. You most commonly see scrub oak right after a wildfire because of the newly opened canopy allowing sunlight to reach the forest floor. They can sprout up as little as several months after a wildlife and can grow up to 20 feet high on rare occasions. Scrub oak differs from regular oak because it doesn't grow nearly as high and oak is more populous in the Pine Barrens over the scrub version.

Currently the pitch pines on Long Island and New Jersey are under attack from a pest known as the Southern Pine Beetle. It has destroyed thousands of acres of trees on our island and has not stopped yet. Once it infests a tree it only has three months to live and the only way to stop an infestation is to cut down a 30 foot radius of healthy trees around it. If you are driving in the Pine Barrens you might see the devastation of this pest along the side of the road.

The Paumanok Path

Another great feature of the Pine Barrens is a 125 mile trail called the Paumanok Path that takes you from Rocky Point all the way to Montauk. The word Paumanok means "eastern Long Island" to the

Algonquin Indians. The path is Long Island's version of the Appalachian Trail that runs through the Appalachian

Mountains of the eastern seaboard. Annually, there is the Paumanok Pursuit which is a 70k race that follows the Pine Barrens portion of the trail. The Paumanok Path can be split up into two parts, the Pine Barrens portion and the eastern section. It all connects but different trail groups are responsible for the different parts. The path is a great way to explore the best parts of the Pine Barrens and beyond, from the ponds to the lakes and to the marshes. The Paumanok Path has it all. It starts at the Rocky Point Pine Barrens Preserve and goes all the way to Montauk State Park right next to the lighthouse. There are many access points for the path allowing you to go for short or long hikes. Part of the path from Montauk to Sag Harbor was inspired after Stephen Talkhouse, a 19th century Montaukett Indian who walked 25-50 miles a day from Montauk to Sag Harbor. Landmarks along his route have been named after him. He died on August 30, 1879 and is buried in Montauk County Park. The path is all in the woods except for road crossings and a few spots in the Hamptons. The Paumanok Path is marked with white blazes on trees or by small signs like the one pictured above. Below is a map representing the general route of the Paumanok Path.

Hiking

So let's get to the hiking. Most of the best hikes are in the eastern part of Suffolk County but Connetquot River State Park is the big exception. This park is the biggest tract of land left out west and is a great place to see the fall foliage from the riverbanks along its many trails. There are many small parks out there on Long Island but this book will only cover the best. Most of the hiking done in this book was on county or state land with a few exceptions such as Nature Conservancy land.

When you are hiking you also have to remember a few things. One of them is knowing how to read the trail blazes so you don't get terribly lost. The trail blazes are two square markers on a tree that tell you which path you are on and which direction to go. The color of the blazes matches the color of the path that you are on and the orientation of them tells you which way to turn. If one blaze is right on top of another or there only is one blaze it means go straight. If the top blaze is to the left, go left, and if it's to the right, go right. It is simple enough to follow if you know what you are doing. The Paumanok Path is blazed with white markers or labeled with small signs that are easy to follow. The Long Island Greenbelt is also marked with white blazes and yellow trails are usually connectors between two paths. If you are going for a longer hike it is important to bring a trail map and know how to read the trail markers.

Left   *Straight*   *Right*

The other thing you have to do is watch out for ticks that may be carrying Lyme disease. Several types of ticks are present on Long Island and they are the American dog tick, the deer tick, and the lone star tick. The dog tick is found all over Long Island but prefers the western end. The dog tick likes the grassy fields and open areas so be sure to stay away from tall grass. These ticks can pass on a rare disease called Rocky Mountain Spotted Fever which can be fatal. The second tick is the deer tick which can transmit bacteria for

Lyme disease. Some people, but not all, have a red bull's eye at the location of the bite. People who have been infected with the disease will show symptoms of fever, headache, and tiredness after a few weeks from being bitten. At the early stage antibiotics can get rid of the disease, but left unchecked it can cause damage to the joints, nerves, and heart. The last tick is the lone star which is the newest to Long Island but even though it cannot transmit Lyme it can still carry other diseases. Lone star ticks are identified by a distinct white dot on the back which is where the name comes from (not the state). In the larvae stage they are sometimes mistakenly called Chiggers. They can be found in great numbers and if you get bitten by them it is a real pain with red dots on your ankles that can itch for over a week. I would avoid places where they are known to be during the months of July to September.

To help avoid these pests stay in the middle of the path and do not go in any grasses. Always wear tick spray and check every once in a while to see if any ticks are on you. Also try to avoid the hot summer months and instead go in the late fall or winter. Wear light colored clothing so you can easily spot the ticks and always take a shower when you get home.

Wildfires in the Pine Barrens

As mentioned before wildfires are very important to the overall health and survival of the Pine

Barrens. Some of the most famous fires in the Pine Barrens are the Sunrise Fire of 1995 and the Crescent Bow Fire of 2012. But there were many more fires before those. Some of the bigger ones were the 1844 fire which burned 24,710 acres, the 1848 which burned 48,185 acres, and the 1862 fire which swept from Smithtown to the area around Brookhaven. Most of these fires were caused by railroads because the embers from the smoke stacks would land on the easily flammable trees. These frequent destructive fires helped shape what the Pine Barrens are today.

The bigger of the two recent fires was the Sunrise Fire which burned more than 6,000 acres of land and happened in late August and into early September. The Sunrise Fire which was aided by perfect conditions for wildfires engulfed both sides of Sunrise Highway, hence its name. The fire cut off the Hamptons from the rest of the island for several days and was fought by firemen from Long Island, NYC, and Connecticut. Almost 25 years later the vegetation has regrown on Sunrise Highway and sprouted new pine and oak trees that will eventually blend in with the surrounding forests. The more recent fire which happened in 2012 in Manorville was called the Crescent Bow Fire and burned around 2,000 acres of Pine Barrens. It caused closure of parts of the LIE and some houses were placed under mandatory evacuation. 109 fire departments helped battle the blaze which was put out relatively quickly. A few firefighters' were surrounded by the blaze and were forced to go into a nearby pond in Robert Cushman Murphy County Park. You can see the burn damage on Wading River Manor Road growing back from after the fire. Sometimes it looks as if nothing had ever happened and that is the beauty of the regeneration of the Pine Barrens.

The Book

This book is laid out in a very easy, simple to use format. I will give you the number of acres of the hike if available, the length of the hike, and the GPS coordinates to the trailhead. The last part is especially useful because some of the parking lots of the hikes are very difficult to find. I also numbered the hikes from the greatest (1) to great (32). Even number 32 (Randall Pond Preserve) is still a wonderful hike. When I was numbering these hikes I had a hard time because they are all great. They all deserve number (1). In the text I laid out what the hike is about and how to follow the trails. Enjoy walking through the deepest secrets of the Long Island Pine Barrens.

1. The Walking Dunes of Hither Hills SP

1,775 acres
¾ mile loop
40°51'23.4"N 72°38'46.7"W

The reason I chose this hike as number one is because the Walking Dunes of Hither Hills State Park are dunes that you would not think have existed on Long Island. They are constantly changing so one year the landscape looks entirely different than another. Strong northwesterly winds have been moving these 80 foot tall dunes for over a hundred years. At the top of some of these mountains of sand you can see for a good distance getting nice views of Napeague Bay and Napeague Harbor in the distance. The reason the dunes move so much is because the wind gets funneled between Gardiners Island and the mainland. These winds are so strong that they move the Walking Dunes 3 ½ feet a year and that's where they get their name from. They move so much a year they bury entire forests under them killing the trees. When the dunes move on they leave behind the remains of the once living forest and expose what is known as the phantom trees. You can see the trees begin to get buried by the approaching mountain of sand on this hike. They appear as shrubs but are really 10-20 feet tall, dwarfed under the approaching dunes. They are moving in a southeasterly direction towards the ocean and will continue in that direction unless stopped by human interference. If you climb to the top of one of these great mountains of sand, please do not tread on any grasses or plants as they keep the sand from eroding. You can see where people have killed the plants making little gullies on the side of the dunes that will slowly erode them.

The plants here are adapted to conserve water in the sandy soil almost like a cactus. One plant you will see is bayberry and it has a waxy coating to prevent water loss. This waxy coating was actually used at one point to make candles. Another plant you will see in great numbers is beach heather which has long roots to absorb the most water and has very pretty flowers in the summer. You also might spot beach plum which is protected from the salt spray by little hairs on its leaves. Its berries are edible and used to make jam. Lastly, a staple of the Pine Barrens is bearberry which grows on mats along the trail. This groundcover also has edible berries and surprisingly grows in the Arctic as well as the Pine Barrens.

If you take this trail you will also pass some cranberry bogs which actually have cranberries growing in them. Also present in these wetlands is a carnivorous plant called the thread leaved sundew. The plant has a main stalk with little hairs and a sticky substance on it that traps flies when they land. The plant will then curl over the fly and digest it for the nitrogen that it can't get from the soil. The last thing I want to mention is

On top of the 80 foot dune

that at the start of the hike right before you enter the woods there is a box with a trail guide. This guide has numbers on it that correspond with various trail markers on the hike. If you stop at a number you can take out the guide and it will give a brief summary of what is there.

So how do you get to the Walking Dunes? Do not be discouraged that this hike is out in Montauk. It is by far 100% worth every minute and is a great place to take kids because it is only a 3/4 mile loop. So if you are coming from the west, take Sunrise Highway all the way east. Continue on Montauk Highway until just before it splits into Old and New Montauk Highway. You will make a left turn onto Napeaque Harbor Road and take it to the end. If you have trouble with these directions use the GPS coordinates given at the beginning of the chapter.

When you get to the trailhead at the end of the road there will be Napeague Harbor to your left and

Hither Hills State Park to your right. At the trailhead you will take a right and proceed on the path towards a big sign talking about the dunes. After the sign you will see the backside of these great dunes on your left and on your right will be a typical Pine Barrens forest. The trail will ascend to the top of the dunes where you can see for miles before descending into the wetlands of the small cranberry bogs scattered throughout. The trail eventually loops back to your car if you follow the trail markers. When I did this hike I went off the loop trail and headed to the top of some of the dunes. I would recommend you do the same because you will never know what you might find lurking behind the 80 foot tall Walking Dunes.

The Hidden Side of Hither Hills

41°00'49.9"N 72°00'24.8"W

The hidden side of Hither Hills State Park is definitely worth checking out. Most people know Hither Hills for its camping which is on the south side of Montauk Highway, but on the north side is 1,775 acres of undisturbed wilderness. There is a large network of trails going to many interesting features such as Nominicks Overlook. This hill, accessed by the Paumanok Path, gives amazing panoramic views of the park. The Paumanok Path also passes Fresh Pond which is fairly large and goes past the sandy beaches of Napeague Bay. To get to the parking lot stay on New Montauk Highway after the road splits and pull into the

Hither Hills West Overlook which has great views looking to the west. It is a fairly big parking lot with a lot of signs giving information about the park. At the far end of the parking lot is where the trails are. There are two paths with one going to the right and the other going left. Left will take you to Fresh Pond and eventually to the Walking Dunes which can be accessed easier on Napeague Harbor Road which was covered in the first part of the chapter. Left can also take you to the Paumanok Path which goes to Nominicks Overlook and along the beaches. Right, however, will go to the eastern portion of the park which has a big kettle hole called the Devil's Cradle. Hither Hills State Park is a great place to go both camping and hiking.

2. The Dwarf Pines (east and west)

290 acres (east side)
6/10 of a mile (east) and up to 5 miles (west)
40°51'46.5"N 72°38'46.6"W (east)
40°51'23.4"N 72°38'46.7"W (west)

The dwarf pines are one of the coolest aspects of the Long Island Pine Barrens because only three places in the world have communities of them. Here, New Jersey, and the Shawangunk Mountains of upstate are the only places where you can find them in the entire world. The dwarf pines have a rank of G1G2 which means they are critically imperiled or imperiled globally and at a very high risk of extinction. So several years ago the dwarf pines of Westhampton were preserved by state and local officials. Recently the county has opened a nature trail on the east side of Old Riverhead Road, just north of the airport in Westhampton. This is a short trail, only six tenths of a mile long, but great for inexperienced hikers. The trail gives an introduction to the rare community of dwarf pines and the interesting flora that thrive there. However if you are adventurous and want to see more, the west side of the road is the better option for you. You will leave the noise of the road and enter a peaceful forest of dwarf pitch pines. The dwarf pines here are generally 3-6 feet in height compared to 20-80 feet in the rest of the Pine Barrens. The reason they are so small is because the soil is poor. The acidic soil allows little water and nutrients to be retained in it, resulting in the dwarf pines. On the east side of the road you will see clumps of reindeer lichen which grows like crazy here. It is a small groundcover plant with white fibers that look like spider webs. What is cool about reindeer lichen is that they have a symbiotic relationship with an algae. The algae gives the lichen carbohydrates and in return the lichen provides nutrients and protection to the algae. Another groundcover on the trail is bearberry which is found in almost all Pine Barrens habitats. It has bright red berries that are edible in the fall. You would think no animals would live in the harsh conditions of the dwarf pines but you're wrong. For example you might see a marsh hawk flying overhead hunting for ground prey or even an owl. Another cool predator that lives in the dwarf pines is the northern harrier hawk, which instead of nesting in trees, nests on the ground. The endangered buck moth also lives in the dwarf pines. They go underground in the summer to be protected from the frequent wildfires in the area and in October, the moths emerge from underground to live a few short days and seek mates. From late morning to early afternoon you can see these black, white, and orange insects take flight. I would highly suggest you stop by in October for the amazing sight. They lay their eggs on scrub oak which is the caterpillars' main source of food when it hatches. Like many things in the dwarf

The dwarf pines of Westhampton

pines, the trees also have a relationship with fire. The pines need the fire because they have serotinus cones which only open during intense heat. Since fire has been suppressed from this ecosystem many times, the dwarf pines won't repopulate and oaks will eventually take over.

You have two options. Either go for the 6/10 mile loop or venture deeper into the woods with the longer hike. If you decide on the shorter loop it will be on the east side of the road, but the parking lot is ironically on the west side of the road across from the Water Authority. It will be a big dirt parking lot that usually has a lot of cars. Since there are no trails right there you have to cross over the road to the Water Authority, and on the right side of the building will be the trail for the dwarf pines. Just follow the path inwards and there will be plenty of trail markers guiding you on the loop. You will see reindeer lichen and huge mats of bearberry lining the path along with many other

Clumps of reindeer lichen growing along the path

plants. Every once in a while will be a sign explaining some natural phenomenon of the rare dwarf pines.

If instead you want to go for the longer hike it will be on the west side of Old Riverhead Road. It is some ways down and easy to miss since it doesn't have an official parking lot, just a gate with a small sign. For this hike I would recommend using the coordinates given at the beginning of the chapter. The path is wide and straight and was once paved but now is crumbling. At the end of the path when it starts to turn right, take a left to go to the even shorter pitch pines from the wildfire of 1995. You can see the vast differences between the dwarf pines and the new pitch pine saplings. Even though they are currently both about the same height, the dwarf pines are much more twisted and developed with years of growth.   Remember to not get lost because the only landmarks are a tower from the airport and a water tower. However if you do get lost, just keep walking in one direction and you will eventually hit a road. There are several small hills that that give you amazing views of an endless sea of green for miles. These hills may not be that tall but are well worth the hike. Don't forget that it gets REALLY HOT in the dwarf pines during the summer so be prepared.

3. Connetquot River State Park

1,743 acres
3 miles to the fish hatchery and back
40°44'53.3"N 73°09'08.4"W

Connetquot River Sate Park is the last big area of undisturbed wilderness in western Suffolk County. With its 3,743 acres and 50 miles of hiking trails it is a great place to visit. It has miles of trails following the pristine Connetquot River, which flows through the park, along with a fish hatchery, a nature center to explore, as well as artesian wells and several bridges that cross over the river. If you stop and take a look you may see the many fish present in the river such as rainbow, brown, and brook trout. The fish hatchery recently reopened and is expected to produce 30 to 35 thousand fish a year which are released into various waterways on the island. The hatchery was closed down in 2008 due to IPN, a contagious disease for fish. Up until now Connetquot River has been stocked from outside sources. The DEC got rid of the disease and the hatchery reopened in early 2017 and is now operating at full capacity. Another interesting feature of Connetquot State Park is that bordering the northern boundary is a small park called Lakeland County Park which is handicap accessible with boardwalks that go for about a mile. The Long Island Greenbelt Trail runs through this park as well as Connetquot State Park and is one of the six greenbelts on Long Island that the LIGTC manages (Long Island Greenbelt Trail Conference). The others are the Nassau-Suffolk Trail, the Walt Whitman Trail, the Long Island Seashore Trail, the Pine Barrens Trail, and the Long Pond Greenbelt (some of which are covered in other chapters). The Long Island Greenbelt is marked with white blazes and goes from Hecksher State Park to Sunken Meadow State Park while passing through Connetquot and Lakeland parks. The LIGTC office is located in Blydenburgh County Park which is covered in another chapter. At Lakeland County Park you will pass Honeysuckle Pond named for the honeysuckles that line its shores. You will also walk through the headwaters of the Connetquot River surrounded by its many wetlands. The Southern Pine Beetle has virtually destroyed every Pitch Pine tree in this park. I saw only one left alive on a recent walk of my own. The boardwalks are also a bit confusing because of the many dead ends but nevertheless it makes a great short walk. To get to Lakeland Park, go on Johnson Avenue in Islandia and it will be on the south side of the road.

So, back to Connetquot State Park. The land for the park was acquired in 1973 from a hunting club called Southside Sportsman's Club. Eventually the land was given to the state and was named Connetquot River State Park with 50 miles of trails. The park entrance is located on the north side of Sunrise

Highway in Oakdale with an entrance fee of $8 dollars per vehicle but it is worth it. Pull past the toll booth and park in the parking lot on the west side of the road. Straight ahead will be the visitor center, trails, and Main Pond which is part of the Connetquot River. There are two ways to get to the fish hatchery and they are the red and yellow trails. I prefer the red path because it is more scenic but the yellow trail gets you there faster. To follow the red trail go to the visitor center and take a right on a bridge going over Main Pond. After that keep left at the fork with several view points of the Connetquot River on your left. At the next fork take another left and you will come up upon a little dock in 500 feet that is an excellent place for fall foliage pictures. Keep following the red trail with many paths crossing over it until you reach the artesian wells on your left with a sign talking about them. Artesian wells are different from regular wells in that the water flows up from the ground without any pump. It flows from just the pressure of the underlying rock above the aquifer. There is an artesian well in Terrell River County Park and many other places on Long Island and in the New Jersey Pine Barrens. Continue past the well and make a left to head towards the hatchery and the river. Once you cross over a small bridge the hatchery will come into sight on the right with all sorts of canals and channels diverted from the Connetquot River. Notice the three sets of pools used to raise the trout with a net over two of them to keep the birds from eating them while they are small. Take a second to look for the

Connetquot River viewed from the bridge

thousands of fish in the water on both sides of the hatchery then head towards the bathroom near the parking area. Past the bathroom, on your right will be a small bridge that in my opinion is the best place on Long Island to look for fall foliage. This bridge makes for perfect pictures down a tributary of the Connetquot River and is a must see for the fall. Past that bridge you will head into the woods where you can cross another beautiful bridge that is worth stopping for. Take a while to explore the hatchery area then turn right to head back on the red trail to the visitor center. But if you want to you should check out Bunces Bridge by heading back to the bathrooms and going on the white greenbelt trail to the north. After passing Bunces Bridge, the Long Island Greenbelt trail will continue all the way to Lakeland County Park and points north. On the west side of the river are many fields that were used by the previous inhabitants of the park, the Sportsman's Club, for hunting small game. These fields are overgrown with tall grass so make sure to stay out of them during tick season which is the summer months. Connetquot State Park has everything to offer from hiking, to cross country skiing, to horseback riding, to fishing, and much more. This state park is a must hit in the fall for Long Island's best fall foliage.

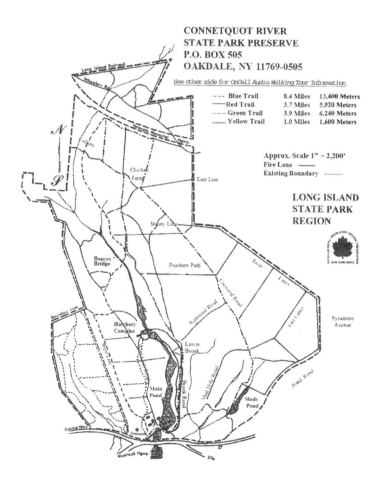

CONNETQUOT RIVER STATE PARK PRESERVE
Sunrise Highway Oakdale-Bohemia, New York 11769

4. Quogue Wildlife Refuge

300 acres
8/10 mile loop, 1.4 mile loop, 3.1 mile loop
40°50'02.4"N 72°36'55.1"W

The Quogue Wildlife Refuge is a great place for people of all ages because it encompasses many different ecosystems accessible by relatively short hikes. The refuge, which was founded in 1934, rescues permanently injured animals from the wild and takes care of them. The animals include bald eagles, owls, falcons, foxes and other species. When you first walk into the refuge, the cages will be on your right with tons of cool creatures in them. However, on your left will be this beautiful cabin overlooking Old Ice Pond. Part of the building overhangs onto the water and on the north side of the cabin are huge windows with rocking chairs looking out onto the pond. On the other side are some stuffed birds and even a live chinchilla which looks like a bunny. The cabin is a great place to start or end your hike and it feels like you are upstate rather than on Long Island.

To get to the refuge, go on Montauk Highway in Quogue and then turn onto Old Main Road. Just stay on this road until you come to the park on the north side of the railroad tracks. When you get to the refuge

The cabin overlooking the waters of Old Ice Pond

you will park on the opposite side of the road and then cross over to the entrance. Walk in and check out the animals or explore the inside of the beautiful cabin. Then, take a look at Old Ice Pond. It was used in the early 1900s as an ice harvesting pond during the cold winters. Then in the 1930s, the Black Duck population decreased and a group of hunters got worried and so they formed the Southampton Township Wildfowl Association. The easterly 104 acres of the former Quogue Ice Company was donated to them by a member of the STWA. In 1938 they purchased the western 107 acres for just $1,400. Finally in the 1980s Southampton Town donated the last 100 acres to the refuge as a result of rezoning.

So let's get to the hike. Continue into the refuge until you hit the big trail map just past the animal cages. There are three different length trails with green

Old Ice Pond

being 8/10 of a mile, yellow being 1.4 miles, and red being 3.1 miles. If you want to go on the green trail go straight, but if you want the red or yellow paths take a right. Even if you decide to take one of these paths there are many connector trails that can shorten or lengthen your hike which is a very nice feature of the refuge. If you take the green loop, you will follow Old Ice Pond to your left for about 500 feet. Then you will take a left onto a boardwalk crossing over the pond. Again, you will take another left following the pond back to the cabin with amazing views through the trees. On the last leg of the trail you will be a on a little causeway that dammed up the pond, since at one point it wasn't a pond at all. It used to be a tidal creek that flowed all the way to the bay. After the causeway you will go on another boardwalk through a little swamp that is prime habitat for turtles. You will then head back to the cabin after an 8/10 mile loop which is great

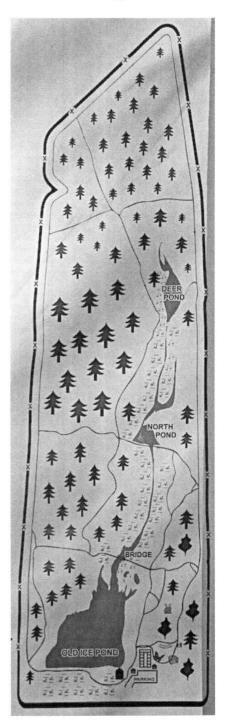

for smaller kids. If you decide to take the yellow loop instead, you will go right at the trailhead and follow the yellow blazes. You will eventually cross over what is called North Pond on a dam where you might see a turtle sunning himself on a log. If you look to the south side of the trail there is a birch tree that people have carved names into. Birch used to be more common on Long Island but since it had many uses it was cut down widespread across the area. You can only find a few places with birch left anymore. After crossing North Pond, the trail will turn south and follow the green and red trails back to the starting point at the cabin. The last path you can take is the red trail, where you will pass everything mentioned before on the green and yellow trails, plus Deer Pond and go into part of the globally rare dwarf pine forest. If you like the dwarf pines do hike number two in Westhampton. This hike is the longest being 3.1 miles long but completely doable. At the end of the refuge property is Gabreski Airport which you can see through the fence.

The reason why I like this hike so much is because it encompasses three ponds, two boardwalks, two dams, animal pens, and the globally rare dwarf pitch pines. It is truly a great place to go to any time of the year. Even in the winter, because the refuge offers cross country skis for rent.

5. Prosser Pines County Park

56 acres
7/10 mile loop
40°52'17.3"N 72°56

The first time I stepped foot into the park my breath was taken away. Even though it was only a small 56 acre park, it was amazing. When you look up to the 100 foot towering white pines it feels like a mini redwood forest that you would not think existed on Long Island. In past years, several hurricanes have knocked down many of the trees in the park but even though this seems bad it actually creates more room and sunlight for younger, healthier trees to grow. If you take this hike you will notice the hundreds of saplings growing in the nourishing light let in by old trees falling down and opening the canopy. This is a natural process that helps the forest stay healthy for future generations. The only sad thing is that the Southern Pine Beetle is at work again. It has destroyed many 200 year old trees and continues to spread. Over 100 foot tall white pines had to be cut down because of this pest, and if it doesn't stop the entire forest could be gone in a matter of years, so get there now.

In 1812 Billy Dayton planted the first white pine seedlings on his farm which would be purchased in later years by George Prosser who the park is named after. Mr. Prosser built a road now called Yaphank Middle Island Road running around the forest so the public could enjoy the trees. Eventually the county purchased the Prosser Estate and turned it into a county park. Lands adjacent to the park that were a former scout camp became Cathedral Pines County Park which is located across the road. Everyone enjoys the pines and one example of that is a poem written in the 1960s by Walter Beverly Crane.

" Of Prosser's dreamy woods I sing.
　　Each tree a harp each branch a string.
　　The cadence soft and low is balm,
　　In Prosser's woods a hallowing calm.
　　Tis God's cathedral, minister choir,
　　The singing pines are harp and lyre;
　　In Prosser's woods I voice a prayer,
　　And worship god and nature there."

As mentioned before, adjacent to Prosser Pines is Cathedral Pines County Park which is located across the street. It also contains some of the huge pines planted long ago but not to the extent seen in Prosser Pines County Park. Cathedral Pines is bigger with 320 acres and six miles of mountain biking trails. There is also camping, playgrounds, sports fields and a few hiking trails but not many.

So let's get back to Prosser Pines. Pull into the dirt parking lot that can hold about ten cars. You will

The white pines are over 200 years old in some cases

see the familiar county park sign at its entrance
bordered by green fence most of the way around. Start
by walking in at the trailhead and you will see a small
map and a bench. You have the choice of either going
left or right but I would recommend going right first
because it starts off more scenic. When you first walk
in, look up and be amazed at the 100 foot pines and
look down at the carpet of needles covering the ground.
I cannot stress enough that it is a beautiful place to be
anytime of the year because the white pines stay green
all the time. Continue right and just meander around in
the 7/10 mile loop. It is very hard to get lost even
though there are many paths crisscrossing around the
56 acre park. Eventually you will come to a sod farm
behind the park on your right. The trail will turn left
away from the farm and approach a make shift teepee
on your left that is quite big. Whenever I do this hike I
do it multiple times because of the short length but it's

your call. At the end take a minute to stop and admire the beauty of Long Island's version of a Redwood forest.

A beautiful picture of the white pines at Prosser Pines

County Park

6. Calverton Ponds Preserve

350 acres
About 2 miles to all the ponds and back
40°53'28.0"N 72°48'23.2"W

The Calverton Ponds Preserve is off the beaten path, but is a jewel of the Pine Barrens. It contains three coastal plains ponds which support the highest concentration of rare species in NYS. The US Fish and Wildlife Service considers these ponds to be of "global significance" for the 26 species of the rare plants, fish, amphibians, moths, butterflies and animals that live there. Also there is half a dozen different bladderworts, threadleaf, and sundew which are all carnivorous plants that are in the ponds. If you visit in the summer you will also be treated to the sweet fragrance of the sweet pepper bush.

What's also unique is that both high and low water levels of the coastal plains ponds are needed. Since the ponds are fed by groundwater and rainfall only, the water levels fluctuate drastically with the seasons. When the water is low it exposes the bare ground for new seed germination and growth. When the water is high, it kills off woody plants that invade from the neighboring pine forest.

So getting to this hike is a bit tricky. It is off the

beaten path on a small road with no real parking lot. The preserve is owned by the Nature Conservancy so you will see a sign for them at the trailhead. Either plug in the GPS coordinates or follow my directions to get to the preserve. If you are going north on Wading River Manor Road in Manorville, after the big bull on the right, turn onto Old River Road and in a few hundred feet it will be on your left. Do not stop at the first gate, but at the second gate. Park on the side of the road and follow the trail inwards and in several hundred feet you have the option of going straight or right. Straight will take you to Sandy Pond and right will go to Block Pond. If you chose to go straight you will come onto a little causeway that was used to dam up Sandy and Block Ponds for cranberries in the 1900s. These cranberry bogs were in operation for 50 years. Long Island was once a very large producer in cranberries which you will find more about if you go on hike 9 at Cranberry Bog County Park. On your left will be some nice outlooks onto Sandy Pond which are worth stopping at and watching for the immense wildlife present here. At the end of the causeway you can go left or right. Left will ultimately lead to a dead end but it brings you to Fox Pond which is the farthest west of the three ponds. If you went in this direction there will be a small path on your left going to Sandy Pond with another beautiful observation point. Past that on you right will be some private property adjacent to the preserve land but you will turn left soon to go to Fox Pond. At Fox Pond, there is the remains of an old dock no longer in use and my guess is it was part of the cranberry bog operation. After you admire the beauty of this pond turn back, but instead of taking a right onto the causeway in a little bit go straight to pass Block Pond. Block Pond is a half marsh, half pond. There are many carnivorous plants in the amazing diverse pond along with sweet pepper bush which gives off a wonderful scent in the summer. Loop back to your car and be sure to check for ticks for they are plentiful. This hidden jewel of the Pine Barrens is secluded deep into the woods bringing out the best of nature. Enjoy!

Block Pond at Calverton Ponds Preserve

7. Wertheim National Wildlife Refuge

2,550 acres
2.5 or 3.4 mile loop
40°47'35.1"N 72°52'47.7"W

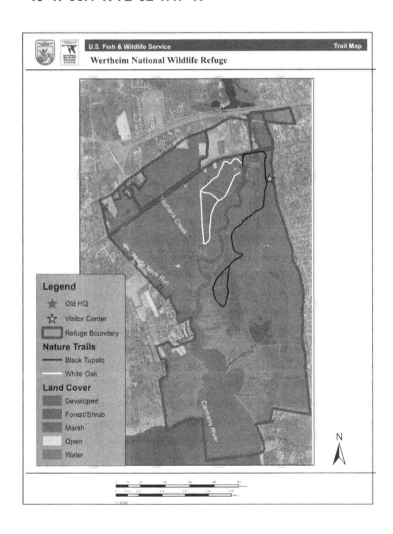

The Wertheim National Wildlife Refuge is the largest national wildlife refuge on Long Island. It hosts the Carman's River which runs through the park until it hits the Great South Bay. The Carman's River is a New York State designated scenic river and is one of the largest on the island. The refuge also has fresh, brackish, and saltwater wetlands. These habitats support white-tailed deer, osprey, muskrat, fox, turtles, frogs and fish. Also present here is the black tupelo tree for which a path was named after on the east side of the river. Black tupelo is one of the oldest species of trees in the area and is capable of living over 650 years.

What's also very interesting is that if you look on satellite images you would notice big ditches in the marshes leading to the river. In the 1930s, these ditches were added to drain the marshes because they thought that would reduce the mosquito population. However, the rainwater still collected in the low areas and the mosquitoes still bred. The small fish that fed on the mosquito larvae could not get into the drier marshes to eat them and so the population actually increased contrary to what they thought. In the 1940s, pesticides were used but damaged the ecosystem. So today the refuge uses what is called Open Marsh Water Management, which is where they refill the marshes with water so it lets the natural predators of mosquitoes back in.

If you visit Wertheim National Wildlife Refuge you might spot a real treat, a bald eagle. The bald eagle was seen last year (2016) in a nest on the White Oak

Trail towards the southern end. These birds are making a real comeback after being gone from Long Island for a while. You also might see eastern box turtles which are quite common at the refuge but are in decline on Long Island. Lastly, you can see some wild turkeys roaming around the woods. Turkeys are making a comeback on Long Island after being hunted to extinction in New York in the mid 1840s. In 1948, the first turkeys crossed over into New York from Pennsylvania. In 1959, a program was begun by the State Conservation Department to trap wild turkeys where they were abundant to be released elsewhere in the state. A typical release consisted of eight to ten females and four to five males. After the first birds were trapped in Allegany State Park, 1,400 turkeys have been moved within New York. When I was younger you rarely saw a turkey on Long Island, but now you can see them all the time on County Road 51 and in Wertheim National Wildlife Refuge.

Have you ever wondered what a turkey eats? Well, they can eat acorns, nuts, flowers, fruits, grains, and can scratch through 4 to 6 inches of snow to find food. Turkeys don't like to fly, but when they do they reach speeds of 40 to 55 miles per hour. They can also swim in water and run up to 25 miles per hour. Turkeys are truly a fascinating bird that are great to have back on the island.

So, how do you get to Wertheim National Wildlife Refuge? Go to Montauk Highway in Shirley and turn onto Smith Road. The parking lot will be on the

The Carman's River at Wertheim NWR during the fall

west side of the road. When you pull in you will notice the visitor center which is fairly new. Inside is a really nice education center along with a mini museum and a gift shop. Outside of the visitor center is a trailhead with two paths, and right behind the trailhead is a boardwalk with a dock at the end of it. If you go to the right of the boardwalk you will be on the White Oak Trail and if you go left of the boardwalk you will be on the Black Tupelo Trail. At the end of the Black Tupelo Trail is Indian Landing which was actually used by the inhabitants of the refuge many hundreds of years ago. The Black Tupelo Trail is a 3.4 mile loop that is partially handi-capped accessible for only 0.3 miles. If you decided to take the White Oak Trail it will be 2.5 mile loop that starts out by crossing an old metal bridge. In the fall it is great to stop on the bridge and see the vibrant colors coming from the oaks lining the Carman's River. The river is also an excellent place to canoe or kayak since it is fairly calm. If you continue you will come across the old headquarters and maintenance area. You have the choice of going straight or right, but since it is a loop it all connects. If you continued straight you will pass over two small creeks that have an abundance of eastern box turtles in them. Their shells are usually brown or black with yellow or orange radiating lines or patterns. Eastern box turtles are really slow movers which results in death by cars very often. The species is labeled at vulnerable which means that unless conditions threatening its survival improve, it will become endangered. Towards the end of the path before it starts to make a loop there is a great lookout onto the beautiful marsh. This is the area where the bald eagle nested last year. Bald eagles tend to nest in the same spot every year but this one hasn't been seen in a while. If you continue you will see tremendous damage done by the southern pine beetle to the pitch pines of the park. Sadly, this pest is killing thousands of pitch pines on Long Island and hasn't stopped yet.

Wertheim National Wildlife Refuge offers beautiful riverside scenery unparalleled on Long Island.

8. Bald Hill County Park

Over 6,000 acres for the "Manorville Hills Area"
About 7/10 of a mile to the top and back
40°52'45.4"N 72°42'20.1"W

I like this hike for many reasons. One is that you climb to the top of a 295 foot "summit", and two, is that there are countless numbers of trails that go into the thousands of acres behind Bald Hill (not the one in Farmingdale). These paths can also take you to 1st, 2nd, and 3rd ponds which took a lot of creativity to name them. They are small but still worth the trip. Ironically, 1st pond is the biggest, followed by 2nd and 3rd ponds. The water level in them fluctuates with the rainfall, so the spring is the best time to see them. But in the summer, sweet pepper bush grows and also many other interesting plants.

Bald Hill is adjacent to Manorville Hills County Park and other state lands which means you can plan endless hikes from County Road 51 to County Road 111. You can take a long but worthwhile hike from the Manorville Hills County Park trailhead all the way to Bald Hill. From different sources you might hear Bald Hill County Park being called Suffolk Hills or even Peconic Hills County Park. I personally believe Bald Hill County Park suits it the best. It is part of the "Manorville

Hills Area" which is a group of land acquisitions made by the county and state. The total land mass of the "Manorville Hills Area" is over 6,000 acres, the largest undeveloped parcel on Long Island. The land stretches from Route 111, to the LIE to Nugent Drive, and to County Road 51.

There are so many places to access this wonderful tract of land, but the only official place to park is Manorville Hills County Park which is covered in another chapter. For this hike, you have to park on the side of Rt. 51 in a dirt pull off. There are also other access points on County Road 51 that can lead you to Bald Hill too. One of them is a big dirt road with a yellow gate that you can take to Hot Water Street which is a wide woods road. Another alternate parking spot is off of Nugent Drive in Riverhead, at the end of a development on the south side of the road. Lastly, you can park on Toppings Path also off of Nugent Drive which runs north to south through Manorville Hills County Park. What I love about Toppings Path is that it serves as a landmark in the midst of the countless acres of woods because you can take it north to Nugent Drive or south to a farm along Rt. 51. What is also great about Bald Hill County Park is that part of the Paumanok Path runs through the area which is a great path to hike on passing the best hills and kettle holes.

So, to get there go on Route 51 from either Riverhead or East Moriches. If you are going south on Rt. 51, after the turn for the college, the pull off will be on your right in about a mile. It is very easy to miss

The view from Bald Hill

since there is nothing marking its existence except a trailhead sign. It is just a wide dirt road going into the woods with a silver gate several feet onto the path. If you are going north on County Road 51, you will see the path on your left after you pass the water authority pump building. Make a u-turn to get back to it. Remember, it is not the woods road with the yellow gate even though you can still take it to Bald Hill. I would recommend using the GPS coordinates since it is hard to miss. Once you get onto the path, it is smooth sailing. In several feet there will be a path going to the right which goes to the ponds I mentioned earlier. If you go right, it will become gradually get less hilly and turn into more pine tree than oaks. But to get to the hill stay straight and soon you will see a sign for Bald Hill. Turn left and you will start your ascent up to the top of the hill. Once there, look on your left and through the trees you can see Riverhead and the court house. The trees are slowly growing back in from a fire long ago so the view gets less and less every year. On the ground is a USGS survey marker back from 1932. You are currently on the Paumanok Path which will take you to many good sights if you wish. You can make a short loop down the other side of the hill or simply turn back. I would recommend exploring the wonders of this place because with 6,000 acres you don't know what you can find.

9. Cranberry Bog County Park

165 acres
1/4 miles to Sweezy Pond and back
40°54'09.4"N 72°40'19.2"W

What you may have not known is that cranberry bogs were once very popular on Long Island. Long Island, in the late 1800s, was the hub of cranberries in the U.S. At one point, Riverhead was producing the third largest crop of cranberries in the nation. When Riverhead was a small town in the 1800s it had to be very self-efficient. It had an advantage because there was a stream to use for water power and so mills were built along the Peconic River. One of them, called Sweezy's Red Grist Mill, was actually powered by the Little River instead of the Peconic. The Little River is an outlet of Wildwood Lake, runs through present day Cranberry Bog County Park, and eventually goes to the Peconic. John Sweezy, who was the owner of the mill, ground grain for the local farmers in the area. He owned the woods and swamps along the river and much of the land around Wildwood Lake.

In 1885, two brothers called the Woodhulls formed a partnership to grow cranberries in the area. They purchased the land from Sweezy but it had to be graded in order to flood it for the cranberries. By

Christmas of 1885, ten acres were prepared for the following spring. Cranberry vines were set in the ground in May of 1886 and in the same year 15 more acres were graded. Thirty five men were employed at $1 a day to help grade the marsh and plant the cranberries. The cranberry vines were purchased from New Jersey and Cape Cod.

The first crop from the vines was in 1889 when only ten bushels were sold locally. However in 1890 ninety bushels were sold at a price of $1.90 per crate. In 1891 the crop was five hundred bushels at $3.25 per crate. Finally, the following year production skyrocketed. They sold 21,600 bushels for $2 each. The bog eventually closed down in the 1900s due to slowing production.

It's amazing that you can still see the remnants of the spray house which was where water was mixed with lime and vitriol to be sprayed onto the bog. This was done to prevent funguses. What's also present on the hike is a bridge that crosses over Sweezy Pond which was where the cranberry operation took place. The bridge is currently closed off because a storm damaged it but it might be open now.

To get to Cranberry Bog County Park, turn onto Lake Avenue in Riverhead. On the west side of the road will be a pullout with a Cranberry Bog Nature Preserve sign. Park into the dirt parking lot and walk in on the once paved road. In 500 feet you will come to Sweezy Pond. You have the option of going left or right on a small path but take a second to look at the pond. You

Bearberry

can see turtles, dragonflies, and carnivorous plants in
the water, but on dry land you might see lichen or
bearberry. These plants like the acidic soil of our sandy
Pine Barrens. Bearberry is a low groundcover with
green, waxy leaves that has berries which are edible in
the summer. The berries are actually very good for you
but I would not advise you to eat them off the side of
the path. Cranberry Bog County Park also has the
largest number of hessel's hairstreak, which is a
butterfly, in the state . There is also carnivorous plants
present that need a way to get nitrogen which the bog
lacks. They use different mechanisms to catch flies and
kill them. One example is the pitcher plant which uses a
pitcher like tube filled with nectar and water. The flies
get attracted to the nectar and go inside, but they
cannot climb out so they are trapped and will die.
When the fly gets stuck, enzymes are secreted and
break down the insect. Another carnivorous plant
present at the bog is the sundew which is quite

Sweezy Pond

different from the pitcher plant. The sundew has a stalk sticking up with reddish hairs that attracts flies. When the fly lands on it, it gets stuck in a sticky substance and the entire stalk curls over the fly and starts to break it down. The sticky stuff on the ends of the stalk glistens in the sunlight giving it its name, the sundew. Some animals that live in the preserve are muskrats, rabbits, white-tailed deer, and garter snakes.   Another interesting is a actually across the street. Cedar Pond and Cheney Pond are cedar swamps which are rare on Long Island because their wood was highly logged during the 1800s. You can't access Cheney Pond and Cedar Pond because it is on the other side of County Rt. 51 and no paths go to it, but you can bushwhack to get there. Sweezy Pond, which is Cranberry Bog County Park, is the largest remaining cedar swamp on Long Island but Cheney Pond and Cedar Pond close in size. Another cool cedar swamp is at Owl Pond in Flanders which you can see on hike 19.   After you hike to

Sweezy Pond, I would advise you to turn around because the paths on the left and right are severely overgrown. If you go in the winter, however, the left path with take you to a bridge and the right path will take you to the remnants of the spray house. Cranberry Bog County Park is a small park with big history.

10. Manorville Hills County Park

Over 6,000 acres for the "Manorville Hills Area"
Up to 9 miles
40°51'42.8"N 72°46'07.7"W

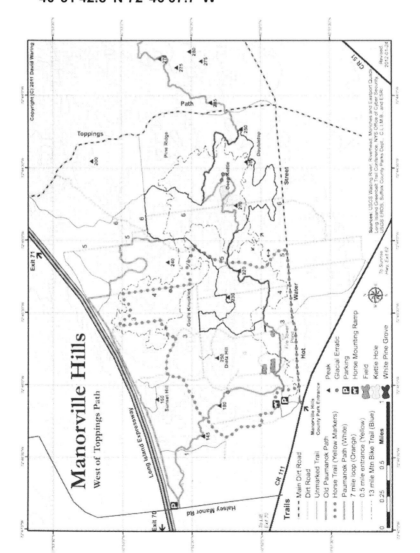

Manorville Hills County Park offers many great features such as mountain biking, horse-back riding, and hiking. There is even a horse-mounting ramp. Manorville Hills County Park by itself is not that big but when it connects with other county park and state lands it totals over 6,000 acres. This assemblage of state and county land together have the largest expanse of roadless land on Long Island which makes for endless hikes in any direction. If you are a serious hiker, this is the place you must absolutely go.

I broke the "Manorville Hills Area" into two parts: Bald Hill County Park and Manorville Hills County Park (Bald Hill County Park is in another chapter). They both border each other and share trail systems. You can cross from county land to state land and back to county land without even knowing it. That is the beauty of the "Manorville Hills Area". It is called Manorville Hills for a reason because it is on the spine of the Ronkonkoma Moraine which makes the terrain very hilly. But in the dips of these hills is what are called kettle holes. The holes were formed by glaciers 22,000 years ago. One of the more famous kettle holes in the park is Deep Kettle which the Paumanok Path goes to. Past Deep Kettle are also two large glacial erratics which are basically big boulders left behind by the glaciers. Glacial erratics make a great place to stop and take a break or eat a snack. Manorville Hills is an excellent place to see the glaciers' impact on Long Island from the kettle holes to the hills, to the erratics. The many hills in the park include Dietz, Sunset, and Doubletop with countless more. Dietz Hill, which is a 1.5 mile hike, offers a semi-nice view from on top. On this hill, there used to be radio towers from the Radio Corporation of America which owned this property, the Sarnoff Preserve, and the Rocky Point Preserve. You can see the remnants of the old radio tower here. Another great hike is to 160 foot Sunset Hill which you can see a very nice sunset from, hence its name. Doubletop is another destination with two tops of almost equal height separated by only a couple yards. Doubletop is the farthest of the hikes in the county park and offers only a decent view, but is still very nice. The last hike I would recommend is going to see Deep Kettle. It takes a while to get there but it is worth it to see the very large kettle hole. You will also pass through a very cool white pine grove towards the beginning of the trail. If you like the white pines, check out Prosser Pines County Park which is hike number 5. I just want to mention that it is easy to get lost in the interior parts of Manorville Hills, so if you do, get to a woods road and walk in any direction and you will eventually come to a road. Hot Water Street and Toppings Path are the two main woods roads in the park. They were made when subdividing the land for a sale a long time ago before turning into a park. The woods roads make for gentle hikes and provide very useful shortcuts for they are mostly straight. Hot Water Street runs from the east to the west and Toppings Path runs from the north to the south. Besides Hot Water Street and Toppings Path there are numerous other woods roads that are

One of the many glacial erratics present along the Paumanok Path

numbered from 1 to 6 which you can reference on the map. Just be warned that the cell phone service in the park is spotty, so make sure you know where you are going. Another feature of the "Manorville Hills Area" is the Paumanok Path. It used to be close to the LIE but got moved farther inland to make for better hiking. When you first walk in past the trailhead, it will go left and straight. If you stay on the Paumanok Path straight, it will take you to Deep Kettle and eventually Bald Hill. But if you take it to the left it will go to the LIE and points west. The path is 9.7 miles long from the Manorville Hills trailhead to the Rt.51 trailhead which really shows the expanse of the area. There are also several fields in the park near the beginning that contain some cool birds and even sometimes turkeys. If you are visiting Manorville Hills for the first time, I would highly recommend taking the Paumanok Path to the east because it winds through some of the finest

Pine Barrens terrain. There are countless hills with good views in the winter and tons of glacial erratics where you can stop and take a rest on. The forest is so pristine because it has been burned so many times which is key to the long term survival of the Pine Barrens. What is also interesting to think about is that every time there is a fire, the tops of the hills open up creating even better views than before. If you take the Paumanok Path past Deep Kettle and past Doubletop you will cross over Toppings Path and into the Eastern Manorville Hills. Along the path in here you can see one of the larger glacial erratics called the Spire and you can climb to the tallest hill in the area, High Hill at 300 feet. Then to top it off you will arrive at Bald Hill with the finest views in the Pine Barrens. For more about Bald Hill visit its chapter.

The parking lot for Manorville Hills County Park will be on Rt. 111 on the east side of the road. The entrance is a bit weird because you go in straight, but then make a sharp turn left. If you kept straight going past a yellow gate that would be Hot water Street going eastbound. You can still park there though and walk around the gate. After you make the sharp turn left, you will make a hard right and in 500 feet on your right will be the parking lot. If you continue to go straight, it takes you to the horse-mounting ramp and then makes a loop back out of the park. At the parking lot, which can only hold 10 cars, there is a trailhead with a very useful map that is put in this book. On the south side of the parking lot is the blue trail that is meant for mountain biking. It is a really nice trail that makes a 13 mile loop around the park. If you are into biking you should also go to the Rocky Point Pine Barrens Preserve which has double black diamond trails. On the north side of the parking lot is the yellow trail that goes into the heart of the park. For the sake of things we are going to hike to Deep Kettle which is a very simple hike. Go in on the yellow trail, and then in a few hundred feet it merges with the white blazed Paumanok Path. You will follow the Paumanok Path all the way to the kettle hole. There will be many side paths but just follow the white blazes. You will come across two fields, and after the second one is a beautiful white pine grove less than an acre big. The path goes right through the towering pines for about 30 feet. After that, it starts to get more hilly climbing to the summit of a 220 foot hill and then to a 270 foot hill. The nameless 200 foot tall hill offers very nice views when the leaves are down in the winter. Right before Deep Kettle is a wide path going north to south. If you feel like it is too hard to make it back the long way, go south along the path until you come to a left and a right. Go right/west and it will take you back to the parking lot faster. At Deep Kettle you will notice the descent downward into the kettle hole, and right afterwards the path pulls out of the hole and continues on. There will be two more glacial erratics after this that you should stop at if you have the energy. If you continue on the Paumanok Path it will take you to many more hills such as Doubletop, High Hill, and eventually Bald Hill. I love to bushwhack (go off the trail) in

Manorville Hills because there are some very neat features that I didn't even know existed. If you are the serious hiker Manorville Hills is the place to go.

11. Montauk State Park

724 acres
3 miles roundtrip
41°04'17.3"N 71°51'33.1"W

       Many of us know Montauk State Park as just the lighthouse. Well you are wrong. You can easily go for at least 5 miles in Montauk State Park and if you connect your hike with Montauk County Park and Camp Hero State Park you can go for several miles more. Since Montauk County Park and Camp Hero State Park will be covered in another chapter I will just talk about Montauk State Park. As with many of these parks the Paumanok Path runs through it and goes to some of the best spots. The Paumanok Path starts near Oyster Pond and eventually goes across the road to neighboring Camp Hero State Park. It follows the shoreline until it ends at the Montauk Lighthouse on the tip of Montauk Point. What's great about Montauk State Park is that there is a pirate legend involved, seal watching, and a lighthouse. The pirate legend revolves around Money Pond which the green trail passes. It is said that treasure was hidden in the "bottomless" Money Pond but to this day no treasure was found. However there was a pirate named Captain William Kidd and he did deposited treasure on nearby Gardiners Island. In 1699, after Kidd's arrest, the money was retrieved from the island but the legend still exists that more treasure is buried at the bottom of Money Pond. During the hike you will pass this pond and also a seal watching site on the north shore of the park.

The most famous feature of Montauk State Park is the lighthouse. It is the fourth oldest active lighthouse in the United States and is a National Historic Landmark. It also was the first lighthouse in the state of New York and was commissioned by George Washington. As of 2017 admission to the lighthouse is $11 for adults, $8 for seniors, and $4 per child. The museum is privately run by the Montauk Historical Society. The tower is 110 feet, 6 inches tall and the light can be seen a distance of 17 nautical miles out into the Atlantic Ocean. Construction of the lighthouse was authorized by George Washington on April 12, 1792 and was completed on November 5, 1796. When the lighthouse was built it was 300 feet from the coast and now it is only 100 feet away due to erosion of the shoreline. The Montauk Lighthouse is made out of sandstone and painted white with a broad red stripe in the middle. If you decide to check out the park I would advise you to go to the top of the lighthouse because the view is amazing.

After you park come back onto the road where the toll booth was. Take this road for about 500 feet and on the right side will be the green trail for Money Pond. It is a good idea to pick up a trail map at the restroom. Do not take the first wide paved path right near the parking lot (the red trail) but the small path with green blazes and a sign saying Money Pond Trail. Follow this trail in and right away will be a nice overlook

looking north towards Block Island Sound. Continue on the green path passing a side trail to your right that goes to the red trail. Eventually, you will reach the highlight of our trip, Money Pond, which will be on your right.

A view of the park from atop the lighthouse

If you keep going you will reach the yellow Seal Haul Out Trail going to the left and right. Left will go to Montauk Highway, a much larger pond called Oyster Pond, and the Paumanok Path. Right will go to the seal observation site and will make a loop back to the car. If you decided to go to Oyster Pond I would highly recommend it because it is at least 20 times the size of Money Pond and much nicer. However, you should continue right to check out a viewing platform for harbor, ringed, and harp seals. Follow the blazes for the yellow trail at the next intersection. You will come out to a really nice viewing area where you can see the migrating seals in late winter to early spring sunning on the many rocks lining the shore. There are several signs talking about the difference between the harbor, ringed, and harp seals and where they go for migration. After you have enjoyed the view, turn back and take a left to follow the red trail all the way back to your car while also passing many nice coastal plants native to Montauk. You can make a great day trip out of this park if you combine the lighthouse with some wonderful trails.

12. Mashomack Preserve

2,039 acres
1.5 miles (red), 3 miles (yellow), 6 miles (green), 10 miles (blue)
41°03'25.0"N 72°19'30.2"W

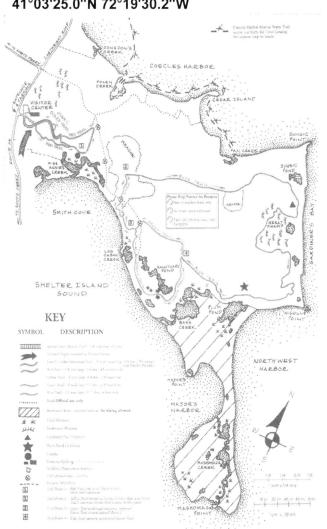

Mashomack Preserve is the jewel of the Peconic Bay with 2,039 acres that encompasses one third of the entire Shelter Island. What's more is that it has a 10 mile loop which is actually quite big for Long Island hiking standards. The blue loop which is the biggest passes fields, swamps, and saltwater marshes along the way while also passing a Gardiners Bay overlook. In the 1600s the inhabitants of the preserve were the Manhansets who were part of the Algonquin Indians. The land was later purchased by the Nature conservancy in 1980. Mashomack Preserve is open 9 AM - 5 PM March through October and 9 AM - 4 PM November through February. The preserve is closed Tuesdays, except in July and August when it is open 7 days/week. In January, the preserve is open only on the weekends so make sure to check the calendar. The preserve also suggests that you give a suggested donation of $3 per adult and $2 per kid to ensure the future of Mashomack. The only downside of this pristine preserve is that it is on an island which means you have to take a ferry from either Greenport or North Haven. The ferry ride is $16 dollars round trip as of 2017 but check their website for the latest information.

Once you get to Shelter Island take Route 114 until you come to a sign for the preserve on the east side of the road. Pull into the parking lot and proceed past the visitor center until you get to the trailhead. Either go left or right on the red trail because they both meet up eventually. The red trail will turn into the yellow path in 3/4 of a mile leading you into some

The marshes at Mashomack Preserve

very nice open fields that are excellent for wildlife viewing. Soon the yellow trail will meet up with the blue and green paths in the middle of the field. If you go to the left you will be on the 10 mile long blue path loop but if you take a right you will be on the shorter 6 mile green loop. If you are an experienced hiker I would recommend the blue path because the views are amazing. There is Plum Pond, Bass Creek, and many other coastal ecosystems to check out. However, if you went on the green trail you will pass over Sanctuary Pond on a very nice boardwalk that has beautiful sunsets. Both the green and blue trails will pass a part of the park that is off limits to hiking. It is called the Katherine Ordway Wildlife Refuge and it protects the unstable, rare, ecosystems of the southern part of the preserve. Mashomack Preserve is called by the Nature Conservancy "one of the richest habitats in the Northeast" which is amazing since it is right here on Long Island. This is a must stop hiking destination if you are visiting the area.

13. Sears Bellows County Park

979 acres
About a 4 mile loop to Sears Pond and back
40°52'45.3"N 72°33'12.9"W

Sears Bellows County Park is in the heart of the Pine Barrens with its two main features being Sears Pond and Bellows Pond. There are five named coastal plains ponds which are Grass Pond, House Pond, Division Pond, Sears Pond, and Bellows Pond with at least 10 unnamed wetlands/ponds. The park also has camping on the lakefront of Bellows Pond for tents and trailers with a small playground nearby. You can rent rowboats for Bellows Pond and fishing is permitted for bluegill, bass, perch and pickerel on the pond. Beyond Sears Bellows County Park is Birch Creek Owl Pond, Maple Swamp, Hubbard, and Munn's Pond County Parks which all connect to make endless hikes. The Paumanok Path is an excellent trail that runs through the park and passes the best sights. The path is blazed with white markers or small signs. Another trail that runs through the park is called the Bay to Bay Trail which you can take south to Shinnecock Bay or north to the Peconic Bay.

To get to Sears Bellows County Park go on Flanders Road and then turn onto Bellows Pond Road at the light, or if you are coming on Montauk Highway turn north onto Bellows Pond Road in Hampton Bays. The entrance will be on the west side of the road with a large county park sign. After you park go towards Bellows Pond but then at the playground take a right following a woods road. You could also take a left at the playground and follow a blue loop around Bellows Pond too. All the ponds found in the park are fed by groundwater and rainwater so the water levels fluctuate drastically with the seasons. The coastal plains ponds are of "global significance" for the endangered species they harbor. What is also neat is that high water levels and low water levels are necessary for the survival of the ecosystem because high levels kill off invading plants from the surroundings and low water allows seed germination.

Walking along the path you might also notice dead pitch pine trees. This is from a pest known as the southern pine beetle which has destroyed thousands of trees on the island. Just south of the park is the greatest concentration of beetle damage on the island where there is literally no pitch pines left. Unless we get a really cold winter this pest will be around for years to come.

Going back to the hike, just stay on the wide trail but notice the many ponds and wetlands through the trees. Once again most of them dry up in the summer but if you get a rainy spell the ponds may actually overflow. You will pass out of the campgrounds

Bellows Pond frozen in January

soon and into classic Pine Barrens habitat with several more small wetlands on your right. Next you will pass what is called House Pond on your right which you can see fairly well through the trees . After passing House Pond the trail will meet up with the Paumanok Path and you have the option of going left or right. Right will take you north across Flanders Road and into Hubbard County Park which has many interesting features that are worth checking out. Left will take you to Sears Pond which is the best of all the ponds. If you go left there will be another fork in the trail in 200 feet with a sign that points Sears Pond to the right. It you want to make a shorter loop back to the car take a left and then another left to follow the blue trail which goes back past Division Pond and eventually circles Bellows Pond in what in my opinion is one of the nicest loops in the area. But if you continue to the right you will pass several more wetlands until you hit Sears Pond which is one of the bigger ponds in the Pine Barrens. In the fall it makes for a spectacular photo with its autumn colors. It is up to you but you can go to the right following the yellow owl blazes on a loop around the pond. The trail goes to the right and you will pass over a small wooden bridge. Keep going to a wide woods road, take a left, and then take another left in 200 feet to follow the white blazes and the Paumanok Path. You will then pass back towards the pond which is now on your left following a white cedar grove which is quite rare on Long Island since white cedar were logged like crazy in past. You will come to the trail you came in on and just take it back the same way to the parking lot. What I love about Sears Bellows is that you can plan long hikes that go through beautiful rolling hills and pass spectacular ponds. You can also connect to Hubbard County Park to the north, Birch Creek Owl Pond County Park to the west, Munn's Pond County Park to the south, and Maple Swamp County Park in the far west (most of these are covered in other chapters). With Sears Bellows County Park being the hub of this area of the Pine Barrens, the hiking possibilities are endless.

14. David A. Sarnoff Preserve

2,749 acres
Red Loop (around 6 miles), Blue Loop (about 4 miles)
40°53'09.7"N 72°38'35.0"W

David A. Sarnoff Preserve is a really nice place to hike in the middle of the Long Island Pine Barrens. The preserve at 2,749 acres can be linked to the east, west, and south to create hikes that seem to go on forever through the hilly terrain. The area has some cool history too that is linked with the Rocky Point State Pine Barrens Preserve. David Sarnoff, who the preserve was named after, was the general manager and president of the RCA corporation which was a pioneer in radio technology. The towers used for radio communication no longer stand in the David A. Sarnoff Preserve but you can still see the concrete remnants of their once massive bases. For the full history of the RCA and its involvement on Long Island visit the Rocky Point State Pine Barrens Preserve chapter (hike 16).

What I love about this hike is that you can access the trails from multiple places on multiple roads making whatever destination you want entirely feasible. The first entrance is at the end of Old Westhampton Road near Wildwood Lake in Riverhead where you can

The David A. Sarnoff parking lot

immediately access the red loop by taking a left. However, I do not prefer this entrance because the trail is a bit overgrown and rarely used. The next two entrances are on Lake Avenue right before the traffic circle. The first one is on your right if you are going north and is just a yellow gate with a connector path that takes you to the red loop in 500 feet. You can then turn left or right because it all makes one big circle. Continuing north on Lake Avenue is a more formal entrance with a paved road going into the park. There is a small parking area where you can pick up the red trail going to the south while passing Frog Pond on your left in about 500 feet. After Frog Pond there will be a fork with the red trail splitting both directions. After deciding which way you want to go on the loop make sure you watch your trail blazes, because there are many paths that you can get lost on in this remote wilderness. If you went left you will eventually come to a paved road which goes to an alternate parking lot right in the heart of the preserve where the radio towers once were. The red trail will cross over the road and continue southward meandering over many different paths until it starts to turn west completing the loop. The red loop is really spectacular but if you aren't up for the full six miles try the four mile blue loop located on the east side of Route 104/Quogue Riverhead Road. If you are coming south from Riverhead, proceed past the first entrance which has a paved road that goes into the heart of the park and keep going to the second entrance with a nice parking lot and kiosk (GPS coordinates listed on previous page). Park here where you can once again access the red loop by going on yellow connector trail to the west. However, if you want the blue loop which passes some nice wetlands go right on the Paumanok Path behind the trail map. In less than a quarter of a mile you will cross over Route 104 and proceed on a nice, wide path going east. Take the first left to connect to the blue loop which will fork in 500 feet where you can go in either direction while passing some small ponds and wetlands. They are usually dried up in the summer but nevertheless are still worth it. If you wanted to take the Paumanok Path to the left behind the trailhead map the terrain will get quite hilly and the path seems to go on forever until you get to Wildwood Lake in Riverhead. This section of the 125 mile Paumanok Path may be the most remote spot in the Pine Barrens where you can walk for miles without seeing anyone. Another interesting hike you can do is take some of the trails south to the dwarf pines just north of Sunrise Highway.

Even though Sunrise Highway seems far away it's not and the dwarf pines make a really memorable hike. For more about the dwarf pines visit chapter 2.   David A. Sarnoff Preserve is great for secluded hikes with some really neat history.

15. Sans Souci County Park

316 acres
2.4 mile loop
40°45'49.2"N 73°03'58.2"W

Sans Souci County Park is an oasis in the midst of Sayville. A 2.4 mile trail passes the Sans Souci Lakes which are a chain of lakes that were dammed up in the 1800s to make cranberry bogs. They were turned into ten separate lakes by small dams which you can still walk across today. They are mostly overgrown except for one or two which offer spectacular views like nowhere else on Long Island.

At Sans Souci County Park there are two main paths, a white and an orange. The white trail goes north of the connector path and the orange trail goes south of the connector path to the lakes. To get to the parking lot go on Broadway Avenue in Sayville and it will be on the east side of the road just 200 feet south of Target. When you first get to the parking lot you will notice how it can only fit about ten cars, so get there early. On the left side of the parking lot is a trail map and at the back is the beginning of a wide trail. This is the connector trail that is about a quarter mile long. Go in on the trail and in about a hundred feet on the left is another path that takes you to the white loop. If you continue straight instead you will see the orange path crossing both sides. If you take it to the left it once again takes you to the white loop. If you go to the right it will take you to the Sans Souci Lakes. The third option is that you stay straight on the wide trail and at the end of the path take a right. When you hit the fence take a left and you will come out to the very end of the lakes. There is a small plank bridge and a big cement pipe draining into the lakes. I do not know its purpose. After the small bridge the trail ends so turn around and head back to the orange trail you saw walking in. Go south on the orange trail which is not as wide as the previous path. It is marked with orange blazes and on your right will be the houses of Broadway Avenue and on your left will be a fence. The Sans Souci Lakes are actually owned by a Girl Scout Camp, not the park. Only the woods adjacent to the lakes are owned by Suffolk County. But from the trail you can still access the lakes and go across the dams. Just keep following the orange trail until you hit a crossroad where you can either go left or straight. I would recommend left because it goes to the lakes faster for if you go straight it will stay in the woods. But at the end it makes one big loop so it doesn't really matter. In a half of a mile you will start to see the lakes on your left and you will come to a beautiful white pine grove which is a perfect spot to check out the water. Right after the grove on your left will be a small overgrown path that takes you out onto the dam which is a nice spot to rest and enjoy the lakes. The picture that you see on the following page was taken from the dam I just mentioned. Notice the many lily pads and even fish in the Sans Souci Lakes. I have seen what I believe to be a bass that was actually quite big. After you come back from the dam you have the option of going either direction on the orange trail. You could go left which takes you into a small field with plenty of birds or just head back the way you came. It is really up to you because they both go back to the original connector trail. Sans Souci is French for "without worry" so I think this park has lived up to its name.

The Sans Souci Lakes (above) and the white pine grove (below)

16. Rocky Point State Pine Barrens Preserve

6,000 acres
8.5 mile loop
40°54'29.1"N 72°55'17.6"W

The Rocky Point State Pine Barrens Preserve is one of the largest parks on Long Island. There is an extensive, and I mean extensive, network of mountain bike trails, hiking trails, and horse trails. This park has everything you need to spend a day exploring its 6,000 acres. The park is also very accessible with three entrances for hiking, three entrances for mountain biking, and two entrances for horse riding. The main parking spot, which is on Rt. 25a, shares all three types of trails making it the hub for mountain biking, hiking, and horse riding. That is why I like to use the entrance designated for hiking only. It is located on Whiskey Road and is only used by hikers. It is the start of the red trail which eventually connects with the blue trail to make an 8.5 mile loop around the park. What is also great about the Rocky Point State Pine Barrens Preserve is that the Paumanok Path starts here. It starts at a trailhead located on 25a west of the school and shopping center. It is the parking spot on the upper left of the trail map on the following page. The Paumanok Path starts by following the blue trail to the end and then the red trail to the south. It then crosses over

Whiskey Road and is now blazed with white markers.
The path enters what is called the Pine Trail Nature

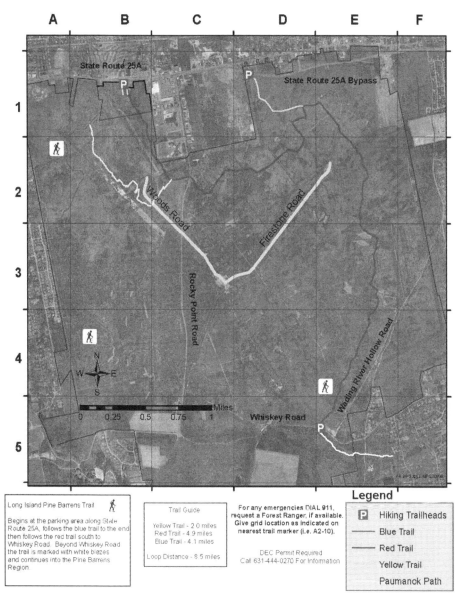

Preserve, which is a long but narrow park that was meant to be a highway before the county bought it.

As mentioned before, there are numerous mountain biking trails within the park. There is a family trail, an intermediate trail, and an advanced trail. Along the 13 mile intermediate loop are several side trails which are double black diamond. These are the advanced trails with challenging uphill climbs and numerous turns. The DEC gives these challenging side trails very interesting names such as Log Jam, Dragon, and Water Bottle Hill. The family trail which is the easiest loop is partially on paved woodland roads while the rest is on wide sandy roads. These trails, shared by hikers, make for a nice relaxing stroll.

To get to the hiking trailhead go on Whiskey Road in Ridge until you come upon a parking lot on the north side of the road. There is a blue horse trail that goes to the left and the right, but for the hike go straight. You are on the red trail right now passing through a fine example of the Pine Barrens. On this trail you will see the rebirth of pitch pine trees after a big wildfire in 1995. During 1995 there were two simultaneous fires, one in Rocky Point and the other in Westhampton. The Rocky Point fire burned 1,800 acres which is about a fifth of the park. You will soon come to an intersection with the blue path going to the left and the red path going straight. If you want to do the full 8.5 mile loop go either direction. Let's say you go left on the blue trail first which will lead you towards Rocky Point Road. It will pass in and out of the burn scars from

A snow covered base of the old radio tower along the blue trail

the 1995 fires with the trees greatly varying in height. In a little less than a mile you will see the old bases of the radio towers lining the side of the trail. The trail will then cross over the road and resume on the other side, starting to turn north. You will soon get out of the pine trees and into a hardwood forest typical of the north shore of the island. There will be a yellow trail going to the right which shaves about a mile off the loop. If you don't go to the right you will stay on the blue path until you reach the parking lot on Rt. 25a where the trail changes from blue to red. Continuing on the red path, the Rocky Point School will be on your left. Shortly you will also pass an old radio tower which the RCA used before the land was turned over to the government. The RCA, or Radio Corporation of America, was the leading company in the radio and TV industry in the early 1900s. The RCA owned many properties on Long Island including the Rocky Point Pine Barrens Preserve and David A Sarnoff Preserve. The Sarnoff Preserve, located in Riverhead, was named after the RCA's general manager and company president. This property was the receiving station and Rocky Point was the transmitting station. The Rocky Point Preserve which housed what was known as Radio Central began construction in 1920. In November, 1921 President Harding pressed a button that officially opened the Radio Central in Rocky Point. Radio Central sent transatlantic radio messages to European countries such as Britain, Poland, Spain, France, and Germany. The facility, at the time, was the largest radio transmitting station in the world. At Radio Central were several buildings used for research on the many ongoing projects at RCA and building #10, which you can still see, housed the laboratory where the first color television was made. The RCA was a monopoly of its time owning NBC and many properties around the United States. Eventually the land was sold to the government for $1 and it became known as the Rocky Point State Pine Barrens Preserve. It is amazing that there is so much history present that no one knew existed right here on our island. What else you may not have known is that the famous inventor, Nikola Tesla, had a laboratory located right in Shoreham on the north shore. It was called the Wardenclyffe Tower and was basically a giant tesla coil intended to give free electricity to people around the world. Eventually Tesla lost his investors and the tower was knocked down, but the building still remains.

After passing the old tower the red trail will cross over Rocky Point Road again meandering through the woods until a yellow path is reached. If you take it to the left, it will lead to another trailhead on Rt. 25a. The red trail will turn south reentering an area with pine trees instead of a hardwood forest. Here you will find many horse and bike paths crossing over the path. Soon the red trail will meet up with the blue trail to the right and the parking lot will be straight ahead on Whiskey Road. The reason this road got its name is because when it was paved the workers were drunk on whiskey and made the road all twisting and curving.

To the south of the road is what's called the demonstration forest where the DEC are actively monitoring and researching the southern pine beetle. The southern pine beetle is an invasive pest that infests pitch pine trees and kills them in as little as three months. It has become a widespread problem on Long Island and without a really cold winter they are here to stay. Even farther south is another portion of the state forest that was acquired from the Baier Lustgarten Nursery which was once the biggest nursery in the state. It is the newest land acquisition added to the preserve with access on Middle Country Road for hiking and horseback riding. It is planned to be part of another greenbelt that stretches from Rocky point through Warblers Woods County Park and all the way to the south shore. Rocky Point State Pine Barrens Preserve is one of the best mountain biking and hiking places on Long Island.

17. Sunken Meadow State Park

1,288 acres
2.5 mile loop
40°54'27.6"N 73°15'14.9"W

Sunken Meadow State Park is a great place for a casual stroll or for longer hikes through the woods. With a very nice 3/4 mile long boardwalk, two bridges, many scenic hiking trails, and a well kept beach, this is the place to go if you are in the area. Although the park is not mostly wooded, a good portion is, making for a very scenic hike from the bluffs. The park also has a waterfront golf course overlooking the sound with 27 holes. Sunken Meadow State Park is also used for cross country running by many local schools and is regarded as one of the toughest courses in the country due to the fittingly named Cardiac Hill and the many ups and downs. The "Sunken Meadow" from which the park got its name is a creek flowing from the sound inland connecting with the Nissequogue River along the way. It isn't a meadow but is sunken between the mainland and the boardwalk, running parallel to the sound. The sunken meadow was dammed up in the 1950s in order to create a park road for visitors but that altered the salinity of the creek. Invasive species started to grow replacing the native saltwater species. But this changed in 2012 when Hurricane Sandy washed out the dam and let the saltwater flow in creating a diverse healthy estuary once again. Sunken Meadow is best seen from the two bridges crossing over it and from the bluffs along the trail. From the bluffs the creek looks like a swirl of sand and water and makes for excellent pictures.

To get to the park go onto the Sunken Meadow Parkway and continue over Sunken Meadow Road. After the big fields on your right take a right before you cross over the bridge. Go on the road to the end and park in parking lot number four. At the beginning of the parking lot is a paved road that continues going east passing a bridge on your left and in 500 feet that crosses over to the boardwalk. In another hundred feet will be another left that takes you on a path to the second bridge crossing over Sunken Meadow. In a little bit the road splits into a fork with a grassy intersection. Take a right going past a cement area with benches. Keep on this until the trail starts to curve and that is where you keep straight going on a much narrower path. You will immediately descend a large hill and then go back up its other side which is part of the reason this is such a difficult cross country course. There will be many ups and downs on this section of the trail but the view on your left of the Sunken Meadow makes up for it. Every once in a while you will come out onto an outcrop affording wonderful views of the Sunken Meadow's colorful waters. The trail will eventually turn right at a large sandy area with access to an alternate parking lot right behind it. After you take a right you will pass through some low brush before coming back out into the open woods. You will take another right with a large glacial erratic on your left in 100 feet that is quite big. In a little bit the St. Johnland nursing home will be seen through the trees on your left before the trail turns away. The path will continue back to the parking lot and I highly suggest you check out the boardwalk and bridges if you didn't do so already. The 3/4 mile long boardwalk is right over either bridge and offers stunning views of the sound with Connecticut in the distance. There is also a snack shop that is open on the weekends on the eastern end of the boardwalk. Sunken Meadow State Park is an excellent place for canoeing or kayaking but is also great for hiking.

Sunken Meadow viewed from the bluffs along the trail

18. Sunken Forest

19,579 acres (Fire Island NS)
1.5 miles
40°43'37.6"N 73°04'20.9"W (ferry parking)

This an AMAZING hike passing rare ecosystems on Fire Island but the only catch is that you need to ride a 20 minute ferry from Sayville to Sailors' Haven. For roundtrip the ferry costs $14.50 for adults, $4.50 for kids, and $2.00 for dogs as of 2017. To get to the ferry which is on River Road use your GPS with the coordinates above or search for Sayville Ferry Service. Parking will cost you $15 on top of the ferry but the hike is so worth it. Take the ferry to Sailors' Haven which is in the heart of Fire Island National Seashore. The national seashore is 26 miles long and was established in 1964. There are 17 private communities within the boundaries of the seashore but no public roads exist, it is only boardwalks or dirt roads. As most of us know, the Fire Island lighthouse is on the western end of the island. To access it you drive across the Robert Moses Causeway and park at the parking lot. You take a small boardwalk trail to the lighthouse which is less than a half mile long. But most people don't know about the Sunken Forest which is sandwiched between the towns of Cherry Grove and Point O' Woods. It contains a 1.5 mile beautiful boardwalk through a 250 year old maritime holly forest. Fire Island supports several ecosystems and they are very evident on the hike. If you go from the ocean inland you will first pass over the primary dune. On these dunes are only the small plants that can tolerant the wind and salt spray. Then you got what is called the swale which is the dip between the primary and secondary dunes. Right behind the secondary dune is where you have the maritime forest. This forest contains hollies, sassafras, shadblow, and many other trees and plants. It is amazing that it takes less than 100 feet to go from the small plants of the swale to the 250 year old trees of the maritime forest. On the trail you will also pass some of the freshwater bogs with phragmites growing around them.

When the ferry docks at Sailors' Haven the first thing you will notice is the visitor center and the snack bar. To the right of these two buildings is a boardwalk trail that goes off into the woods. There is a large national park sign pointing you in the right direction. If you need the bathroom or want to check out the ocean go straight on the boardwalk but the Sunken Forest is to the right. Once you go into the forest you lose any semblance of the beach behind. The canopy grows overhead and now you are in a full blown forest in the heart of a barrier island. In 100 feet you will get a glimpse of the bay to your right but that is the last you will see of it for a while. Continue on the boardwalk and soon you will get to a freshwater bog on your right with phragmites and cattails growing around its shore. After that it starts to get even cooler as you approach the 250 year old hollies. You then will come to a big wooden deck under the canopy. The

The deck with hollies

wooden deck has holes in it with hollies growing through them and there are plenty of benches so sit down and enjoy the sight. You now have two options, go left or go straight. Going left will cut your hike shorter but since it is only 1.5 miles I went with the longer version. You will reach the bay again and the boardwalk splits off to go out to it. Check it out and then head back following the boardwalk to the south until you start to descend out of the maritime forest and into the swale. When you come out it feels like you're transported because the ecosystem is completely different. In the summer when the plants flower it looks wonderful and the sight will take your breath away. The boardwalk will then cross over a sand road and turn into concrete. Continue on the cement until you hit another boardwalk going left and right. To the right is a staircase going down to the ocean and to the left goes back to the big deck with the hollies sticking out of it. To get to the ferry continue straight on the concrete path through the swale. Notice on your right the primary dunes which block most of the wind making it very calm. In over a half mile you will reach the restrooms where you can head back to the ferry. The Sunken Forest at Fire Island is a great hike that will take your breath away.

The entrance to the Secondary Dune/Maritime Forest (above) and the Swale (below)

19. The Maple Swamp Area

Unknown acres
4 miles to Maple Swamp and back
40°53'55.3"N 72°35'22.5"W

The Maple Swamp Area, a relatively unknown place, is a great place to hike for extended distances. It is a secluded spot in Flanders with many trails that go to small ponds or swamps. The park is in the heart of the Pine Barrens so dress warm in the winter because temperatures can plummet. The Maple Swamp Area is an assemblage of parks that feature rare habitats such as red maple swamps and cedar groves. The parks also contain the Paumanok Path which goes past some of the best sights in the area. The Maple Swamp Area is divided into five different parks that are Sears Bellows County Park, Birch Creek Owl Pond County Park, Munn's Pond County Park, Hubbard County Park, and Maple Swamp County Park. All five of these parks are next to each other and are virtually borderless. What I love about this area is that you can walk from Sears Bellows County Park (which is covered in another chapter) all the way to Maple Swamp County Park without even knowing it.

If you are coming from the west, at Riverhead, turn onto Flanders Road. After passing the Big Duck you will have about 2 miles to go. After the road turns to woods on both sides you will pass a tidal creek going across the road. Turn right immediately after the creek onto Spinney Road which is paved for only a few yards. The trailhead will be on your right with a very good map and information kiosk. If you are coming from the east go off Sunrise Highway onto Flanders Road. Take a left onto Spinney Road and the trailhead will once again be on your right.

To the east of Spinney Road is Sears Bellows County Park and to the west is Birch Creek Owl Pond County Park. At the trailhead you have the option to go into the woods on the yellow trail or continue on the road in front of you. No cars are allowed down the rest of the road, so it will make a nice hike that goes all the way to Sunrise Highway and Flanders Hill. But this hike goes in past the trailhead to the right following yellow owl blazes. Keep on this trail and in a half a mile you will reach Owl Pond, which is one of the prettiest ponds in the Pine Barrens. Owl Pond has a white cedar grove growing around it which prefers this habitat. White cedar groves are rare on Long Island ever since it was highly logged in the 1800s for its wood. Since this hike is a loop you have the option of going left or right at the pond so pick either direction. If you went left you are now on the Paumanok Path following the white blazes. The Paumanok Path, which you can learn about in the introduction of the book, is a 125 mile trail that runs from Rocky Point to Montauk and passes the best sights in the Pine Barrens.

Owl Pond

You will soon come to an intersection with a yellow trail to your right. Take this trail and once again you will come to another intersection. Take a left onto the Paumanok Path and now you will be following white blazes again. You will stay on this trail for quite a bit, meandering through the heart of the Pine Barrens. In order to truly appreciate the Pine Barrens you have to notice the subtle details such as small pine saplings regrowing from a brush fire that occurred in the late 1990s. Some pitch pine cones will only open up during intense heat which makes the ecosystem actually very dependent on fire. You will now be passing out of Birch Creek Owl Pond CP and into Maple Swamp CP. Right before you get to Maple Swamp you will be on a high point of the trail where you get a very nice view of the swamp. Once you descend the hill this will be the turnaround point. But take a minute to admire its beauty. Governor George Pataki hiked here in 1996 to

Maple Swamp

check out Maple Swamp and he was so impressed he preserved it for years to come. Maple Swamp is the biggest red maple swamp in the Pine Barrens and has a very unique ecosystem. The swamp is so close to the water table it stays wet all year and never dries up. It is home to various frogs and birds such as the warbler which is a favorite for bird watchers. Maple Swamp is one of the few red maple swamps left on Long Island which is quite sad since there used to be many more. After you admired Maple Swamp turn around and head back on the Paumanok Path. Follow the trail all the way back to the intersection but instead of taking a right on the yellow path keep straight on the white path. In less than a half a mile you will approach Birch Creek which is a tidal creek that flows into the Peconic Bay. Stay on the white markers of the Paumanok Path and when you get back to Owl Pond take a left on the yellow trail to get back. This park is a great place to experience the

Pine Barrens but is a bit hard to find if you are not from the area.

20. Wildwood State Park

600 acres
1.8 miles (red), 2.2 miles (orange), 2.9 miles (blue), 3.7 miles (yellow)
40°57'51.0"N 72°48'08.4"W

Most people know Wildwood State Park for its camping but it has much more to offer. In its 600 acres it has a 3.7 mile trail that rambles through a hardwood forest and goes along 200 foot tall bluffs. The forest at Wildwood is unlike the Pine Barrens because there are only a few pine trees. Instead, there are many beech and oaks. Present are also many chipmunks, squirrel, and deer that roam in the forest. At Wildwood you can swim from 6/25 to 9/5 and camp from 4/1 to 10/10. The camp site at Wildwood is especially nice with paved roads that are great to bike ride on. There are also many picnic tables, a camp store, a playground, and a refreshment stand at the beach. I would recommend camping here because it is one of the better state parks on the island.

To get to the park go north on Hulse Landing Road in Wading River until you see a sign for Wildwood. Take a right and head into the park passing the toll both with fields on you right and picnic areas on your left until you hit the parking lot. After you get you get out of your car head back to the mouth of the parking lot and there will be a trail map on the left. It will show the four different trails with their lengths and where you are. If you want the blue or yellow trails take a left or a right. If you want the orange or red trails head into the woods on the old road in front of you. The trails will be marked with little colored squares on the trees and there will be a map every once in a while on the path. If you want to get to the beach follow the yellow and blue trails left and instead of making a right in 500 feet, stay straight and head down a steep slope to the water. My favorite trail is the yellow path because it is the longest and offers a lookout over the 200 foot bluffs. On this trail you also pass very old beech trees that you don't see much of on Long Island. All four of the trails are on wide paths but just be warned that the trail is very grassy with a lot of ticks so keep checking. The orange and red trails pass through the campgrounds and it is easy to get lost so keep an eye out for the markers or take this book with the map in it. You can spend an entire day hiking in the campgrounds because they are so big. The blue and yellow trails go past a grove of white pines that is being destroyed by the Southern Pine Beetle on either side of the path. These pines, I believe, were on the edge of farmland at one point. About half of the trees are dead in the grove. Wildwood State park is a great hardwood forest park with more than meets the eye.

The beach at Wildwood State Park

21. Southaven County Park

1,356 acres
About a 2 mile loop to the dam and back
40°48'08.2"N 72°53'33.0"W

The jewel of Southaven County Park is the Carmans River which flows for several miles throughout the park. The river is an excellent place for canoeing or kayaking and Southaven even offers rowboat rentals for the day. You can also fish for trout which are quite plentiful in the picturesque river.   Most of the park is on the west side of the river but on the east side is a narrow strip that is used for both trailer and tent camping. You can access both sides of the river by crossing over a concrete dam and is a great spot for fishing and nature viewing. Southaven really has all you need to spend the night camping or just go hiking for a few hours.

To get to Southaven County Park go on the Sunrise Service Road or what is called Victory Avenue in Brookhaven. The entrance will be on the north side of the road surrounded by a green fence. Pull in with the ranger headquarters on the left and a beautiful white pine grove growing on either side of the road. Although the pines are not quite as big or old as the ones in Prosser Pines County Park they are still very magnificent. However, like most other places on Long Island the southern pine beetle is killing many of these trees as we speak. When you hike on some of the trails farther into the park the community of pine trees are decimated by this pest. The southern pine beetle is a big problem that will continue to spread unless stopped.

Right after the white pine grove will be a small pond called Weeks Pond with its tributary running underneath the road. The pond is very pretty and there is a nice trail that goes around its shores with benches to stop and admire nature. What makes it even better is that the white pines are lining the shore making the pond look like something from far upstate. I would highly recommend you stop by Weeks Pond after you park. After you pass the pond on your right will be the tollbooth where you have to pay on weekends in the summer. Then you will come out onto the big parking field that can hold about 500 cars. To the right of the parking field is a path that goes down to the river and to the canoe/rowboat launch site. The trail also takes you to the northern part of the white pine grove and gives you access to Weeks Pond. If you like the white pines you should really check out Prosser Pine County Park (hike 5). To the north of the parking lot is the path that goes to the dam which is an excellent fishing site and an easy hiking goal. Go on this trail until you hit a big, wide road going to the left and right. But instead of taking a left or right, go across the road to another path. On this path take the first right and follow it all the way until

A view of the Carmans River from the dam

the end where you come out onto the dam. Across the dam is the campground and the other side of the Carmans River which has some nice paths that are worth checking out also. But if you're not up to it this is your turnaround point so head back on the path you came in on. You might see a type of Japanese deer called the sika deer roaming around which are native to Asia but have been introduced into the United States and other places around the world. They are slightly smaller than white tailed deer and have spots on their brown to black coat their whole life. Their mating call reminds me of a caribou's because they make the same screechy sound. Keep an eye out for them in the park for they are plentiful.

Once you get back to the car you should check out the Long Island Live Streamers if it happens to be a Sunday. The steamers are open alternating Sundays from May to October and for more information check out their website called longislandlivesteamers.org. They are located within the park are have been operating since 1966. The LILS is a club that has "public run days" where you can ride lifelike scale models of real trains around a 4,600 foot track. There are two tracks with one called the ground line and the other called the high line. The high line is slightly elevated off of the ground but is not as long as the other track. The hobbyists who run the trains are really into it and make it as lifelike as possible with mini railroad crossing signs and other elements. It is a great place to take small kids or even adults on the weekend.

The last thing Southaven has to offer is a trap and skeet range on the western edge of the park. It is a bit noisy but it still doesn't take away from the beauty of the parkland. Southaven County Park is great because from horseback riding to hiking and fishing it has it all.

22. Morton National Wildlife Refuge

187 acres
1.2 miles to observation deck and back
40°59'12.4"N 72°22'09.2"W

The Morton National Wildlife Refuge is a 187 acre peninsula located in Noyack. It is famous for the birds, that are so used to humans being around, eat right out of your hands. You are allowed to bring bird seed but you cannot leave it on the trail for it brings unwanted pests. Dogs are not allowed in the refuge but it is a great place to take kids on a casual 1.2 mile stroll through the woods of the east end. Present at the refuge are all sorts of wildlife ranging from turkeys to birds and to chipmunks that are all tolerant of humans. At the northern end of the refuge is an observation deck overlooking the waters of the Peconic Bay and behind that is what is called Jessups Neck that juts out into the water for about two miles. This long peninsula is an excellent breeding ground for migratory birds and that is why some parts of the beach are closed during portions of the year. The land that the refuge owns was donated by the Morton family on December 27, 1954 and will be around for years to come. Adjacent to the refuge is Clam Island County Park which is at the end of Noyac Bay Avenue and has saltwater marshes and

A bird that will actually land on your hand

coastal habitats.

To get to the refuge go on Noyac Road until you come across a big brown sign on the north side of the road. Pull in to the refuge parking lot which is gated after hours and then proceed to the visitor center and bathrooms. Go past the visitor center on the main trail and stop every once in a while to let the birds land on your hand and eat the bird seed. It is really amazing and makes for great pictures. Just behind the refuge buildings you can either go straight or turn right because they both end up in the same place eventually. I am going to go right because it follows the boardwalks first and passes a small pond. It is really hard to get lost because it is just a loop that goes to a beach but make sure to avoid popular times because they bring many school trips to the refuge. After you pass around the pond the trail will turn left and meet up with the main trail and so take a right to go to the beach. The trail is pretty much straight after this and it will open up to the

Peconic Bay in 1,500 feet with a well built observation deck with several binoculars. This is your turn around point but feel free to continue along the beaches of Jessup Neck and search for the numerous ospreys that nest on the high poles in the distance. There is also a very small burial ground about halfway along the peninsula that is very hard to find but is also very interesting. Morton National Wildlife Refuge is the ONLY place on Long Island where birds eat out of your own hands. I definitely recommend this place to anyone up for a 1.2 mile hike.

23. Robert Cushman Murphy County Park

2,200 acres

This is by far one of the most confusing but beautiful parks I have been to. There is no real entrance but 12 named ponds, the Peconic river, and countless miles of Pine Barrens habitat within its boundaries. The reason this hike did not rank higher is because it is very hard to get to this hidden wonder. It contains the greatest concentration of coastal plains ponds on Long Island and was the county's first natural park. It was named after Robert Cushman Murphy who was a well known scientist who worked at the American Museum of Natural History. He was an advocate against the destruction of Pine Barrens habitat and so a parcel of land was named after him with the highest concentration of coastal plains ponds. The 12 named ponds are Horn Pond, Round Pond, Peasys Pond, Duck Pond, Woodchoppers Pond, Sandy Pond, Grassy Pond, Twin Ponds, Cryan Pond, Zeeks Pond, Kents Pond, and Jones Pond. Those are just the ponds in the western part of the park which has the most trails. However, there are many more ponds in the eastern part of the park. To make this less confusing I am going to divide the area into five sections. The first section is the western section, the second is the middle section, the third is the cranberry bogs, the fourth is the eastern section, and the fifth is the Pine Barrens Information Center.

Western Section

About 2 miles to Sandy Pond and back
40°52'57.3"N 72°49'35.9"W

This is my favorite part of the park because there are at least 4 entrances to the western section which makes for countless different hikes in any direction. The most formal entrance is not at Robert Cushman Murphy County Park but rather at Pine Trail Nature Preserve located off of Middle Country Road in Ridge. It is out of the way from the ponds and goes behind houses so I rarely use this entrance. The Paumanok Path goes through the Pine Trail Nature Preserve and into Robert Cushman Murphy County Park to Sandy and Grassy Ponds. The next entrance is off of Schultz Road in Manorville. It is on the west side of the road with nothing marking its existence except a small path. This path is the Paumanok Path and if you take it west, it will lead you to the two best ponds which are Sandy and Grassy Pond. However, the path also crosses the road and if you take it to the east you will go past the Peconic River and eventually keep going until you get to Manorville Hills County Park. The next entrance is on Middle Country Road, across from Panamoka Trail (a street). It is a small dirt pullout with a gate and a wide trail going into the woods. This trail is good because it passes the upper ponds such as Horn, Round, and Peasys Pond. The last entrance is to the south on North Street. To get there go on North Street and on the north side of the road is a wide path with a metal bar going across. The purpose of the bar is to prevent people from driving in there but it is perfectly legal to walk past the gate. Once you go in, on your right will be a dilapidated house after you cross over the Peconic River. This trail will take you to the southern ponds like Zeeks, Cyran, and Kents Ponds. You can also continue past them to the upper ponds as well. The entrance that I would recommend is the one on the west side of Schultz Road near the burns scars of the 2012 fire. It will be right after a small patch of houses and is easy to miss. As mentioned before, this is the Paumanok Path and it goes on both sides of the road. Use the GPS coordinates to get to the trail. Once you head in on the path you will see the first pond on your left called Jones Pond. It is fairly large with a small path that goes down to its shores. On your right you will see the burn scars from the wildfire of 2012. It is remarkable how well the scrub oak and pine trees are growing back. Pitch Pines are actually very resilient to fire and need it for the species to survive. Fire opens up their pine cones and spreads the seeds that thrive in the nutrient rich ash after the fire. Also a pitch pine's protective bark protects it from fire and the tree can come back even if all the green is burned off because most of a pitch pine's energy is in the roots. When you look to your right you will see the trunks are badly burnt but the

The "toothpicks" of Robert Cushman Murphy County Park

trees are still thriving in the newly opened canopy.

The path you are on is called the Paumanok Path and it is marked with white trail blazes. Soon, on your left will be two identical ponds called Twin Ponds which are small but pretty. After Twin Ponds you will come to a wide open field on your right in about 200 feet. At the end of the field is the option of going left or right. Left will go to Twin Ponds and right will go to Sandy, Grassy, and other ponds. Go right still following the field. In 50 feet you can go either left, straight, or right. Go left but notice that on the path straight ahead all of the dead trees lining the path look like toothpicks. It resembles a tornado but it was just a wildfire that helps the forest in the long run. Following the white blazes you will get out of the burn scars and head into a healthy forest with Grassy Pond poking through the trees on the left. At the next crossroads take a left to

The beauty of the regeneration of the Pine Barrens after a fire

follow the Paumanok Path. There will be a small field on the left with another trail that goes to the shore of the pond. It is a nice place to stop and relax since there is a bench overlooking the water. Go back to the main trail and continue on it until the Paumanok Path turns left into the woods. It will go to a small bridge that crosses over a small stream that links Sandy and Grassy Pond together. However, most of the time it is dried up. If you keep on this trail you will eventually reach Pine Trail Nature Preserve which is an alternate parking spot. If, instead of following the Paumanok Path to the left you stayed straight, you will come across Sandy Pond which is slightly smaller than Grassy Pond. This is your turnaround point if you are tired but feel free to check out the other ponds to the north because there are so many paths and ponds you don't know what you will find.

Middle Section

1.5 miles to Linus Pond and back
40°54'16.1"N 72°49'01.5"W

This is another great spot to hike because it contains 4 coastal plains ponds that are in close vicinity to the parking area. The entrance is on Grumman Boulevard in Calverton with a brown sign saying Preston Pond fishing access site. It is a gravel pullout with a trail leading into the woods on the left. The trail comes out to an open field and turns right following it. At the end of the field is Preston Pond which is fairly large. Take a left and with the field on your left, continue to another unnamed pond. After that stay straight on the main path until you come to an intersection with the choices of going left or right. Take a right and you will see Forest Pond in 200 feet. Just stay on this path until you come to another field with Linus Pond on your left which is the biggest and best pond. If you continue past the field there is another entrance on Wading River Manor Road but is not as nice as the one you came in on. The southern entrance is only a dirt road with yellow bar which you see In many hiking spots on Long Island. This means it is used by hunters but makes for a great hiking trail. You should not use these paths in the winter for it is hunting season. The middle section of Robert Cushman Murphy County Park is nice but I like the western section the best.

The Cranberry Bogs

About a mile there and back
40°53'41.5"N 72°47'39.7"W

This section of the park passes by the cranberry bogs which were formerly the Davis Bogs. The Davis Bogs were the last commercial cranberry bog on Long Island when it ceased operation in 1974. The bogs that you will walk past on your right are full of orchids, which flower in June through July, cattails, and many carnivorous plants. The bogs are shaped like banana if you looked at them on a map and are only a half a mile long. I would recommend this hike in the winter only because the trail is a bit overgrown but is still worth the hike. To get to the trail go on River Road in Calverton. If you are coming from the east 66 acre Swan Pond will be on you right with a small pullout that goes to its shores. Continue past Swan Pond and the trail will be on your left going into the woods right next to the bog. If you pass the golf course on your right you went too far. If you are coming from the west on River Road go past the golf course and right after the bog on the right will be the path. Do not think that the path west of the bogs is it because that goes to private property. The trail is to the east. Once on the path go into the woods following the bogs on your right. The trail gets a bit narrow but widens up later. In a quarter of a mile you can cross over the bogs but the trail on the other side fizzles out. Keep going straight until the end of the bogs where the trail turns into the woods. Don't take the first trail you see but the second one because this will go to a very pretty lookout over the Peconic River. If you want to you can follow the trail for about a mile east until you get to a sporting club. Turn around and head back to the car. Enjoy!

The Eastern Section

2.5 miles from the parking lot to the other parking lot and back
40°54'01.9"N 72°46'25.5"W

This part of the park is the most official but I also think it is the least interesting. But nevertheless it makes a very nice hike through a typical Pine Barrens forest. You also pass by the Peconic River on the trail which flows through most of Robert Cushman Murphy County Park. To get to the hike you will park on either Connecticut Avenue or Grumman Boulevard. Both entrances have a canoe launch into the Peconic River a few feet from the parking lot. To get to the Connecticut Avenue entrance go on Connecticut Avenue in Manorville until you see a brown sign that says Otis G. Pike Preserve. Park here and cross over the railroad tracks onto the trail. A path to your left will go down to the river but a small trail to your right will venture deep into the woods. Go to the right and in a few feet the trail forks. Take a left and this path will go into a typical Pine Barrens habitat that is very secluded and not many people know about. In about a quarter of a mile you will come out to a sandy, open space which has been destroyed by illegal ATVs. Take a left and in 300 feet you will cross over the Peconic River which flows under your feet. It is a bit hard to see through the trees but take a second to look and you might see a canoer every once in a while. If you keep straight you come out onto Grumman Boulevard which is an alternate entrance to the park. The parking lot is a nice, big gravel pullout with another trail that goes down to the river which is a great spot to launch a canoe or admire the beauty of the Peconic River. If you take a left on the boulevard it will bring you to the western section of Robert Cushman Murphy County Park.

Pine Barrens Information Center

About 2 miles to the Paumanok Path and back
40°52'22.5"N 72°48'20.1"W

The Pine Barrens Information Center is located on Rt. 111 in Manorville on the east side of the road. It is a small building with exhibits inside about the Pine Barrens. It is only open Friday-Monday from May to October but the trails behind it are always open. These trails are very nice and connect to the Paumanok Path in Manorville. The trail starts out behind houses and next to power lines but soon goes into the woods. There are several benches along the trail and you can make a short loop back to the visitor center if you want a quick hike. If you want a longer hike keep going until you get to Mill Road where you can pick up the

Paumanok Path going east or west. Follow the white blazes to keep going or turn around and head back to the information center. Robert Cushman Murphy County Park is a great place to go for an avid hiker. However, I would not recommend it for a light stroll.

24. Blydenburgh County Park

627 acres
5.4 miles around the pond
40°49'30.8"N 73°13'28.1"W (south)
40°50'43.5"N 73°13'24.8"W (north)

Blydenburgh County Park is a surprising 627 acres in the middle of Smithtown with a huge lake present called Stump Pond. Also Caleb Smith State Park borders it with 543 acres totaling the two parks at 1, 170 acres. That's a lot of acres to explore! At Blydenburgh County Park you will pass Stump Pond, the highlight of the park. At Stump Pond you can fish for pumpkinseed, sunfish, large-mouth bass, perch and bluegill. You can also rent rowboats from mid May to Labor Day. What else is great about this park is that it has several entrances and a 5.4 mile long trail looping the pond. It is a Greenbelt trail maintained by the Long Island Greenbelt Trail Conference who have an office/gift shop at the park. The LIGTC is an organization that has created over 200 miles of trails on Long Island. Most of them are in western Suffolk but a few are in eastern Suffolk such as the Pine Barrens Trail which is the part of the Paumanok Path that goes from Rocky Point to Westhampton. There is also the Long Pond Greenbelt trail in Sag Harbor that passes several beautiful ponds.

So, I would personally park in the northern parking lot which is at the end of New Mill Road in Smithtown. This is because the Greenbelt gift shop is right here and Stump Pond is only a little ways away. If you park at the southern entrance which is the main entrance you have to go through campgrounds to get to the pond, but it's your choice. The southern entrance also has picnicking, rowboat rentals, and restrooms. However at that entrance you have to pay, whereas the northern one you do not. At the end of New Mill road you will see a sign for the park and a green fence. Pull in and park on the left in a dirt parking lot. In front of the parking lot is the Greenbelt Office and gift shop in an old historic house. To get to Stump Pond continue straight on the road you came in on. On your right will be some wetlands of the Nissequogue River that drains from Stump Pond. In 500 feet you will reach the shore of a beautiful, pristine pond filled with ducks and people row boating. You will see many people fishing on the shoreline for the pond is well stocked with fish. Stump Pond is a bit weird as it is shaped like a big upside down L but that also contributes to its beauty. If you are up for the whole loop you can either go left or right. Since it doesn't really matter I will go left. You are on the Greenbelt trail with white blazes heading east. You stay along the pond for a while with openings in the trees every once in a while. The trail is shared by horses so watch out because I have encountered many on the trail. Soon the trail turns left away from the pond into

Skunk Cabbage

the woods. On this part of the trail are many chipmunks, birds, and a peculiar plant called Skunk Cabbage. Skunk Cabbage has big green leaves that flower in the spring and smells like skunk. This plant is found in great numbers around wetlands and bogs.

In over a half mile you will reach Brookside Drive after passing through some Russian Olives usually filled with all kinds of birds. At the road is another parking lot that you do not have to pay at. This is a good place to park except the buildings are pretty far away. Instead of going out into the road, turn right and you will pass over a bridge with a stream underneath that connects to Stump Pond. The houses and road will be on your left and the woods on your right. In about 500 feet the trail diverges to your left and right. Right will take you close to the pond and left will take you to the restrooms, picnic area, and pavilion. If you want to loop around the pond stay to the right. You will eventually pass a rowboat rental station and past that the path connects with the main road for the south entrance. You will only be walking on the paved road for a brief time because the path goes back into the woods. The trail then crosses over some bridges and boardwalks before heading back to your starting point. Take an occasional side path to see the secluded waters of Stump Pond from different vantage points. Blydenburgh County Park is an extremely nice place to canoe or go hiking in western Long Island.

Stump Pond

25. Shadmoor State Park

99 acres
1.5 mile loop
41°02'26.5"N 71°55'60.0"W

      Shadmoor State Park which was created in 2000 is a great place to explore the Montauk Moorlands. The shad part was named for the numerous shadbush that grow there and the moor was named for the Montauk Moorlands which is a habitat of low growing vegetation in acidic soil. What I love about Shadmoor is that at almost all times you can see above the vegetation on the trail towards the ocean making for beautiful scenery. The park was purchased for $17.7 million with the cost split between the state, the town of East Hampton, Suffolk County, and The Nature Conservancy.

      To get to the park go on Montauk Highway in Montauk until you see a big brown sign for Shadmoor State Park which will be on the south side of the road. Pull into the dirt parking lot which does not charge for parking. Proceed past the kiosk with the trail map and head into the woods. In several hundred feet you can either go straight or to the right. Right will take you on the Roosevelt Run trail which makes a 1.5 mile loop. If you stay straight on Shad Lane it will take you on a

The hoodoos from the beach

shortcut to the beach in about .4 miles. If you decided
to take the loop trail you will be on a straight path going
into the moorlands of Montauk. Take a look at all of the
Shadbush that grows here which are in the rose family.
In less than a half a mile there will be a path on your left
going to a coastal observation bunker that was used in
WWII to look for approaching Nazis from the sea. It has
long been decommissioned but the building still stands.
There were many similar buildings in nearby Camp Hero
State Park which is described in another chapter.
Continue back to the Roosevelt Run loop trail which is
blazed with red markers and soon the vegetation will
open up and you can see the ocean not too far ahead.
It is a very beautiful sight that you would not want to
miss. Once you reach the edge of the bluff overlooking
the Atlantic Ocean there will be a sign explaining the
hoodoos which are rare on the island. The only other
places that I know have them are Hallock State Park
Preserve and Camp Hero State Park. The hoodoos are
geologic formations that have huge spires which are up

to 50 feet tall. They are formed when the edge of the bluff erodes from the rain and melting snow. Hoodoos are common elsewhere besides Long Island in places such as Bryce Canyon National Park in Utah. Robert Cushman Murphy called these huge spires Long Island's "badland topography". There is a place called Badlands National Park in South Dakota which has very similar geographic formations. Here in Shadmoor you can see the hoodoos a little by looking down but if you want to see them fully you have to keep going on the path until you can get access to the beach. The trail turns to the left following the hoodoos on you right with several spectacular lookouts. In a quarter of a mile the Roosevelt Run Trail goes left making a loop back but if you continue straight you can gain access to the hoodoos from the beach. If you want to do this keep going and you will pass over a small bridge with a little creek flowing through it that eventually empties out into the ocean. You will then ascend a big hill with rose bushes lining it the whole way with a great lookout at the top. After descending the hill will be a little path to the right that goes to the beach. On the beach if you head in the direction you just came from will be a ground view from the hoodoos. It is an entirely different prospective from the ground rather than the top. It is a really spectacular sight. Head back to the trail that you came from. To the right on the trail will take you to Rheinstein Estate Park and an alternate entrance. Left will take you back to the main parking lot. Go left until you get to the red markers for the

Roosevelt Run Trail and turn right. Follow these markers back to the parking lot or stay on the big wide road called Shad Lane. Shad Lane passes another WWII building and takes you back quicker. Shadmoor is definitely worth the stop if you are vacationing in Montauk.

A view of the hoodoos from the Roosevelt Run Trail

26. Montauk County Park

1,073 acres
About a 3.5 mile loop around Big Reed Pond
41°04'17.5"N 71°55'04.4"W

Montauk County Park is one of those places that are easily overlooked by the many other parks in the area. Sandwiched between Lake Montauk and Montauk State Park is a little known park that is actually quite big at 1,073 acres and quite beautiful. The star of the show is a very big pond called Big Reed Pond which was designated at as National Natural Landmark in 1973. The pond itself is freshwater but the surrounding wetlands are brackish making a very fragile ecosystem between the two types of water. What else you may not know about Montauk County Park is that it was the site of the first cattle ranch in the entire country that was established in 1658. It has been operating continuously ever since with several concerts in the 1990s featuring Jimmy Buffet and other singers. Montauk was a great place to have a ranch because there was plenty of grass and the surrounding peninsula boxed in the cattle naturally. There were three houses built by the men who tended the animals by the names of 1st, 2nd, and 3rd Houses. Only the 2nd and 3rd house still stand today with only the latter located within the

The 3rd house at Montauk County Park

park. The 3rd house was famous since it was where Theodore Roosevelt stayed in 1898 with the Rough Riders returning from the Spanish American War. They were quarantined since they contracted various diseases from fighting the war. That's why this park is sometimes called Theodore Roosevelt County Park instead of Montauk County Park. To get to the historic 3rd house, picnic areas, and the beautiful horse pastures and ranch go on Montauk Highway all the way past the town of Montauk until you come to a sign on your left for it. Pull in, park in the parking lot, and enjoy the amazing views of the horse pastures before checking out the 3rd house. Afterwards if you want to go hiking you actually have to go out of the park and backtrack a little. Go back west on Montauk Highway and turn onto East Lake Drive and continue to the park sign on the right hand side of the road. It is a small dirt parking lot with a trail leading into the shrub vegetation of Montauk. Take this trail and you will see a side path on your right in about 200 feet that will take you on the opposite side of Big Reed Pond. It doesn't matter which way you go since we will be making a loop but I usually go straight on the wider trail that will take you to the spectacular views of Big Reed Pond on your left. The trail will get sandier with many small paths off to the side that gives really nice views of the pond. The trail will fork soon and you will take a right to continue around Big Reed Pond passing through the small shrubs of Montauk. Take the next left if you want to get back or stay straight to proceed to Quadam's Hill which has amazing views of the lighthouse in the distance. If you went left to get back take the first right and then the first left to get on the trail back to the parking lot. You will eventually end up at the little side path about 200 feet into the hike. Montauk County Park definitely should not be overlooked.

27. Brookhaven State Park

1,638 acres
Blue (1.7 mile loop), Red (3.7 mile loop), Green (5.3 mile loop)
40°54'47.3"N 72°52'43.6"W

Brookhaven State Park is one of the places that most people pass by not even knowing it existed with 1,638 acres of typical Pine Barrens habitat and several ponds. Brookhaven State Park is a nice, secluded place that you can get away from it all and into the forest. The main entrance is on the east side of William Floyd Parkway in Ridge and closes after dusk. The park is open for hiking only on the weekends which I don't understand the reason for, but you can still get around the gate even on weekdays. Just park on the side of the road and walk in.

To get to Brookhaven State Park go on William Floyd Parkway and the entrance will be on the east side of the road right across from Whiskey Road. Pull in and notice the red trail to the left and the blue and green trails to the right. Park in the parking lot on the right hand side of the road and decide which trail you want to use. The blue loop, which is the shortest, is only 1.7 miles long, the red loop is 3.7 miles long, and the green loop is 5.3 miles long. Across from the parking lot is a kiosk with maps that are available for taking. All three trails start out to the right of the kiosk but they loop back to the parking lot in different places. After you decided which path you want to take, head into the woods on a wide path. You will pass a field on your right shortly which used to have picnic tables. In 1,000 feet there will be a bench and a fork in the road. Straight will take you on the red loop and right will go to the blue and green loops. For this hike I am going to do the green loop so stay to the right. In a half a mile the blue trail loop will diverge off to the right and head back to the parking lot. Soon you will pass through the burn scars of a wildfire from the 1980s that burned a good chunk of the park. In another half a mile the Brookhaven Trail crosses over the path which is a 5 mile one way trail that goes from Shoreham Wading River School to the Paumanok Path in Robert Cushman Murphy County Park. It was originally intended to run all the way to the south shore but the Brookhaven Lab would not let the path cross over their property. You will soon cross under a high voltage power line and continue past that until you take a right following the green trail. To your left will be two small ponds that connect to Lake Panamoka and several trails will lead you past these ponds to the road. The road is called the Lakeside Trail and across the street is Lake Panamoka which is really big. Stay on the green trail, where you will turn right passing another pond called Tarkill Pond on your left. It is a nice pond but the power lines cross over it, ruining it a bit. Tarkill Pond is a coastal plains

Tarkill Pond partially dried up during the summer months

pond which means that it is fed by rainwater and groundwater only. Coastal plains ponds provide habitats for dozens of rare species and so they are considered "of global significance". Just south of Brookhaven State Park is the greatest concentration of these ponds which are at Robert Cushman Murphy County Park. Although the ponds may not be that big, the beauty of them in unsurpassed by anything else in the pine Barrens.

Continue across the power lines and pick up the green trail again passing another small pond on your left which is sometimes dried up. One rainy year Tarkill Pond and this pond overflowed so much, they actually connected. Soon you will pass over the Brookhaven Trail again and then the green path will turn south reentering the burn area again. Soon, you will come within sight of Middle Country Road where it turns to the right following a little used road that goes to a firefighter training facility. The green trail will follow this for quite some time and will eventually turn left picking up the blue trail. Then follow the blazes back to the car. What I love about Brookhaven State Park is that it has nice, wide woods roads that limit tick exposure and not many people use them, making a nice, secluded hike.

28. Camp Hero State Park

415 acres
2 miles from the parking lot to radar tower
41°03'54.1"N 71°51'45.0"W

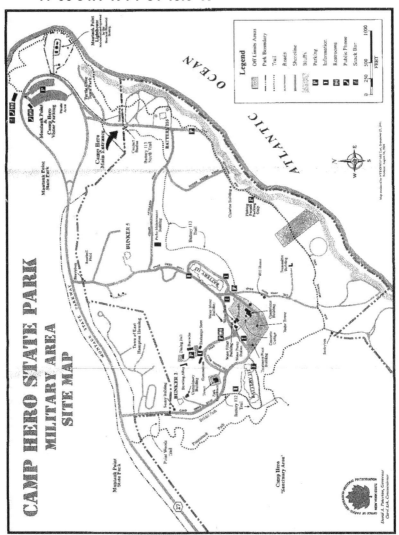

Camp Hero State Park offers more than just stunning views of the Atlantic Ocean, it gives you amazing history that is found right here on Long Island. You will learn the history of the Montauk Air Force Base that was commissioned in 1942 to protect Long Island from invasion by sea. The first radar tower was put up in 1948 to guard the area from surprise attack by Soviet bombers or missiles but in 1960 it was replaced by the one you can still see today. It was called the AN/FPS-35 and was operational until 1980. Another thing you can see at Camp Hero are what are called batteries. There were three batteries built that go by the names of 112, 113, and 216. Batteries 112 and 113 contained two 16 inch guns that were over 600 feet long and made of reinforced concrete. However, the slightly smaller Battery 216 only had a 6 inch gun. You can still see them today but the guns had been removed in 1949. All that is left is a huge concrete bunker that at one point was self sufficient with its own power, water, and ventilation. Also present at Camp Hero are a ton of old buildings from when it was an Air Force Base. These buildings include a dining hall, bowling alley, gym, and barracks. Sadly, they are all boarded up but at one point they were actually disguised to look like a small fishing town so no one would notice from the ocean. For example the gym was actually made to look like a church. Lastly, there have been many conspiracies about Camp Hero saying that crazy experiments were preformed here but there is no such evidence.

There are only three marked trails at Camp

Hero, the Paumanok Path, the Battery 112 trail, and the Battery 113, but there are a bunch of old roads that are nice to walk on too. To get to the parking lot go on Montauk Highway all the way to Montauk Point right before the lighthouse. Take a right at the sign for Camp Hero State Park and continue past the toll booth where you have to pay eight dollars but thankfully the parking pass is also good for Montauk State Park. Right before a dirt parking lot will be a road that goes to the right and if you wish to do less walking and bypass the scenic bluffs, take this road and proceed to the end where it forks. Take a left at the fork and then take a left again to come to a parking lot with a picnic area right next to it. Battery 113 will be right there and so will the radar tower and all the old buildings. At the south end of the parking lot you can also pick up the Battery 113 trail that goes through the woods and eventually ends up at the toll booth where you came in.

The alternate parking lot, which is at the end of the road you drove in on, is a big dirt lot with spectacular views of the Atlantic Ocean below. You can see the Montauk Lighthouse to the left which you can walk to via the Paumanok Path going east. Instead, take a right on a wide dirt road that follows the Paumanok Path to the west for a short while. If you wish to, take a left to keep on the white blazes that will go into the woods about a half a mile into the hike. This will take you to some bluffs and eventually to Battery 112 and picnic areas. If you do not want to go on the smaller overgrown Paumanok Path, stay on the wide

The old radar tower at Camp Hero State Park

road and take the next right. Continue on this road until you get to the parking lot mentioned earlier where you can see all the old military buildings. If you want to access Battery 112 take a left at the fork in the road and go past the radar tower until the path appears on your left. The battery 112 trail connects with the Paumanok Path which you can take north into Montauk State and County Parks. Camp Hero State Park is an amazing place to hike and learn about Long Island's important role in WWII and the Cold War.

29. Terrell River County Park

263 acres
2 ⅔ mile loop
40°47'59.9"N 72°46'31.9"W

This hike offers beautiful views of pristine Terrell River and Moriches Bay. Originally the Havens Estate, Terrell River is now a wonderful place to hike in an oak forest transitioning to pines. The Havens House across the street used to own this property and was farmed up until the 1980s in some spots. The park is an excellent example of farmland returning back to its natural state. The trail at Terrell River County Park features several lookouts of Terrell River and a sandy beach of Moriches Bay. It is one of my favorite hikes since I live close by but get there early because the park draws crowds. The locals use the very popular park for hiking, jogging, and bird watching.

To get there go on Montauk highway in Center Moriches. If you are coming from the east Terrell will be on your left across from Kahlers Pond Park. If you are coming from the west it will be on your right. At the green and white sign pull into the dirt parking lot. If you plan on going there on a weekend, remember, get there early because the parking lot is small and fills up easily. This park is one of the busiest I have seen on the island

and for good reasons. Whenever I drive by there is always at least one car there. At the end of the parking lot is a trailhead with a map where you have the option of going left or right. I would go left first because it follows the river and less people generally use it. The trail is blazed with white trail markers and is very hard to get lost on. In a short bit the trail diverges and you can either take a left or right but it really doesn't matter since they both end up in the same place. You will continue on the white trail and eventually Terrell River will come into sight on your left. It is not technically a river but a deep tidal creek that flows from Moriches Bay to Kahlers Pond. After a while on your right you will pass a pipe coming up from the ground with freshwater flowing out of it. It is called an artesian well and it comes from the aquifers that our Pine Barrens help protect. It is different from a regular well because the water flows naturally from the aquifer because of the pressure pushing it up. Soon, you will come to a crossroads with a picnic bench to the right. You can either take a left or a right but I would advise taking a left because it follows the river. Right can either cut your loop short or be used as an alternate path to access the beach. If you took the left, in a quarter of a mile the trail splits again. If you want to, go on the trail that goes to the river and you will come out onto a scenic lookout in 500 feet with a bench. Take a look at the cattails and phragmites of the river along with the many ducks and geese. Across the river you can see an old duck farm that used to be very common on the

Looking into Terrell River from the peninsula

island and from where the Long Island Ducks got their name. Backtrack to the intersection and continue on the white trail southward. Eventually you will come out to a beach overlooking Moriches Bay. There are two benches for you to stop and take a rest but if you want to you should also check out a very cool peninsula to your left. The peninsula crosses halfway into Terrell River making it a nice, scenic place to stop at take excellent sunset pictures. Across Moriches Bay you can see Dune Road on the barrier island and the many houses on it with the occasional boat in the water. After you are done go back to the bench and head back into the woods. If you keep straight at the bench you will pass another artesian well shortly on you right with a lot of moss growing on it. This path is wider than the one that you took in and you will continue on it all the way back to the parking lot. Terrell River County Park is a great hike for the locals but it offers great views that are worth the drive.

30. West Hills County Park

854 acres
depending on destination up to 4 miles
40°48'04.7"N 73°25'17.4"W

West Hills County Park has nice trails and many entrances making it very easy to get to any destination you want. At the main parking lot is also a dog park and a picnic area currently under renovation. One of the trails in the park is named after the famous poet Walt Whitman who was born only about ten minutes away from the park. The trail is called the Walt Whitman trail and goes to the highest point on Long Island, Jayne's Hill, which is located on the northern end of the park. Jayne's Hill has an elevation of 400.9 feet and was the site of where Walt Whitman visited in 1881. He said "I write this back again at West Hills on a high elevation of Jayne's Hill. . . . A view of thirty of forty, or even fifty or more miles, especially to the east and south and southwest: the Atlantic Ocean to the latter points in the distance - a glimpse or so of Long Island Sound to the north." Jayne's Hill used to be a great spot to look all the way to the shore from the center of the island but now the trees have grown back and obscured the view. There is also a water tower on top of the hill plus a rock reciting the poem of Walt

The rock with Walt Whitman's poem "Paumanok" on it

Whitman called Paumanok. Jayne's Hill is a bit disappointing so if you want some more panoramic views head over to Bald Hill in Riverhead (hike 8).

To get to the main entrance go on Sweet Hollow Road in Melville and the parking lot will be on the east side with a dog park for big dogs. To get to the trailhead walk towards the dog park but then take a left into the woods on a small path. When walking in West Hills County Park try to stay on the wide horse trails because the regular hiking paths are a bit small and ticky. You can continue into the woods and then take a left onto the Walt Whitman trail If you desire to go to Jayne's Hill.

The second place where you can park is on Highhold Drive off of Mt. Misery Road. There is a dog park for small dogs as well as some nice fields and picnic areas. You can take some of the many paths south into the woods but there are not too many sights to see on this side of the park and Jayne's Hill is far away.

The last place you can park is at the end of Mt. Misery Road where you can access some really wide horse trails that are excellent for hiking. These trails can lead you eventually to Jayne's Hill if you stay on the Walt Whitman Trail but it gets pretty close to the Northern State Parkway which takes away from the hike.

Finally, if you are lazy you can get to Jayne's Hill without any hiking by going to the end of Reservoir Road and parking on the side. You walk for about 100 feet on a concrete walkway up to the top of the hill while also passing the water tower. The increase in elevation is very minimal and not strenuous at all. When you get to the top take a minute to admire the hill and then either keep going on the trail or head back. West Hills County Park has nice trails but I would recommend a hike further up the list if you are not from the area.

31. Warbler Woods County Park

750 acres
3 miles from Yaphank Middle Island Rd. to Longwood Rd. and back
40°51'01.9"N 72°56'14.5"W

Warbler Woods County Park was acquired in the 1990s and with 750 acres it is fairly large. The park has many paths making it very easy to get lost but that also allows every corner of the woods to be explored. There are no officially marked trails, only ATV trails, but recently the Long Island Greenbelt Trail Coalition has decided to make a greenbelt run from Rocky Point to Wertheim National Wildlife Refuge. Although this is not yet official it is likely to happen in the next couple of years. This is due to a new housing development on the southeast side of the property that would allow the residents of the soon to be condos to have access to the hiking trails. I think this is a great idea that will bring more attention to Warbler Woods County Park. The Greenbelt is only possible due to a new land acquisition made by the Rocky Point State Pine Barrens Preserve from an old nursery. This new parcel will connect Rocky Point and Warbler Woods together, completing the Greenbelt trail.

Warbler Woods County Park got its name from

the many warblers that migrate during the spring and fall. These very colorful birds are small in size but are a nice sight to see. To get to the park, take Yaphank Middle Island Road until you reach a Verizon building on the east side. Right next to the building is the pullout and sign for Warbler Woods County Park. This is the main entrance but you can also access the park from the end of Shannon Boulevard and on Longwood Road.

Upon entering, the trail will split to the left and right. Right will take you to the southern part of the park and left will take you to the northern part and two small ponds. You will notice it start to get very hilly with some of the hills reaching 190 feet in height. For this hike I am going to go left and in 500 feet take another left. Follow this path until you get to the end where it goes in either direction and right in front of you will be a small, quaint pond. The pond is shallow and vegetation is growing in around the pond/swamp but it is still very nice. Notice how the trees resemble the north shore rather than the Pine Barrens but this will change as we continue. Go to the right on a wide trail which will take you all the way down to a second pond that is much larger. This pond has many spring peepers and is worth the stop. Just behind the pond is a really wide woods road which you can take left to Longwood Road or right to a compost company and a new housing development in about a mile. The new development in which has begun construction used to be the Par Meadows Race Track. It is a great place to explore. Also nearby is a compost company and a large field used for archery hunting. Hunting is permitted November 1st to December 30th so stay out during that time. To get to Longwood Road turn left and continue past a sewage treatment plant on the right owned by the nearby condominiums. In about 3/4 of a mile you will reach Longwood Road which is your turnaround point and an alternate parking area. Warbler Woods is a great secluded hike with the chance of observing unique wildlife and warblers.

The soon to be Greenbelt Trail

32. Randall Pond Preserve

184 aces
3 mile loop
40°53'47.6"N 72°53'29.9"W

Randall Pond Preserve with its 184 acres is a nice place that relatively few people know about. It is located off of Randall Road, just north of the Sunoco gas station on Route 25 in Ridge. When you spot the small brown sign saying the Ridge Conservation Area pull in on the paved road and you'll see a small wetland on your left and buildings to the right. These buildings are hunter check-in stations to check game taken from DEC properties on Long Island. Park in the dirt parking lot and head back towards the entrance and you will see a bunch of trailhead signs on the left. There will be four huge signs explaining things from wildlife to displaying maps for other DEC properties. Continue past them and the trail will start out grassy but soon turns to dirt. In 200 feet on your right, you will reach the first boardwalk that leads out onto the four acre pond. For such a small pond it is surprising that there are largemouth bass, bluegill, pumpkinseed, brown bullhead, and rainbow trout. Continue back to the path and keep going until you see a similar boardwalk on your right again. This one is the best boardwalks giving you a panoramic view of Randall Pond. Notice the many lily pads lining the surface of the pond and you might even see a painted or box turtle sunning itself on a log. Also at this pond are an abundance of bullfrogs on the shoreline. When I went here I saw at least ten of these very big frogs which made for great pictures. Go back to the main path and continue until the trail splits to the left and right. Left will keep on the red trail and right will only go to the road. If you go left you will start your ascent uphill and soon will have a choice to make. To take the red trail and cut your loop short go left which will take you through some old farms reverting to forest. This is called succession and it happens all the time in nature. The grass and shrubs are a great habitat for quail and pheasant which are present here. However, right will go on the blue trail completing the full 3 mile loop. The blue trail also has a side trail that goes to the Ridge Elementary School which is an alternate parking lot. Randall Pond Preserve is a great place to observe a plethora of wildlife.

Hidden Bullfrog in picture

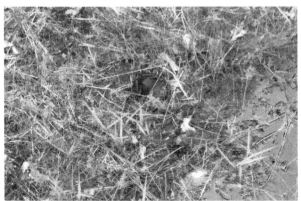

Other Parks of Interest

There are many other parks on Long Island that are not in the top 32 but still deserve recognition. The first one is **Pine Meadows County Park** on County Rd. 51. It is on the east side of the road right after the sod farm and has the usual county park sign. Follow the path inwards and on you right will be a pine meadow like the name, and on your left will be a pine-oak forest. It is a two mile trail to the end and back with additional paths that lead into the woods.

Another park of interest is the **South Shore Nature Center** in East Islip. It is off of Bayview Avenue and is owned by the town of Islip. When you pull in there will be a big dirt parking lot with a kiosk and past that is the visitor center which has live bunnies and a bunch of stuffed animals. To the left of the visitor center is a small pond with a bench but just past

The South Shore Nature Center

that is a network of boardwalk trails that add up to a loop of 2.5 miles through pristine saltwater marshes. Some parts of the boardwalk closer to the bay were destroyed by Hurricane Sandy but still are walkable. It is a really nice loop trail with the chance of seeing of seeing all sorts of wildlife ranging from ospreys to numerous deer, and even muskrats.

Napeague State Park is a little known state park out in Montauk. It is actually very large with 1,364 acres but is quite limited in trails for it only has a 2 mile loop trail and the Paumanok Path. The park is divided into two halves separated by Montauk Highway and railroad tracks. The only trail to the north is the Paumanok Path which follows the railroad tracks but to the south is a 2 mile loop trail called the Oceanfront Nature Trail made by Mike Bottini of the east end. It is a small path that is a bit overgrown but passes beautiful dunes filled with beach heather and bearberry. Access is on the south side of the road with a small sign saying

The dunes of Napeague (above)

Napeague Access Road. Pull into the small pullout and there will be a big, sandy path straight ahead that is for driving on the beach. Instead, go left on the trail following the markers.

There is a small county park preserve called **Munn's Pond County Park** that is located on the north side of Montauk Highway in Hampton Bays. It features a small nature center with animal cages and a small pond called Munn's Pond. The county park land connects with Henry's Hollow State Pine Barrens Forest to the west and Sears Bellows to the north. This has been the site of immense Southern Pine Beetle damage and the DEC had to take down literally thousands of Pitch Pine trees. They have thankfully stopped the spread of the SPB but it still ravishes adjacent forests and preserves. To get to the trail go behind the nature center on a wide path. Follow this all the way to the end until you get to an odd structure that appeared to be a piece of Sunrise Highway that was never built. Go through the tunnel and you will eventually hit Bellows Pond road where you will cross under Sunrise Highway and enter into Sears Bellows County Park.

Cedar Point County Park which is located in Northwest Harbor is an excellent place for camping and hiking. Its entrance is on Alewife Brook Road with the usual county park sign. Drive in on the paved road passing a newly constructed toll booth where you have to pay a fee. Past that on your left through the trees is Alewife Pond which is great for canoeing or fishing. Next, you will pass campgrounds on both sides of the road and a playground after that. Park there and continue down past the buildings on a trail that goes to the beach. Following the trail you will come to Cedar Point Lighthouse which is closed down temporarily due to vandalism. Notice the many cedars that grow on the peninsula that the lighthouse is on, hence the name Cedar Point.

Another park is called **Peconic Bog County Park** but has no real entrance except a path at the end of South River Road in Riverhead. You follow a wide path inwards with the Peconic River on your left and the woods on your right. In a hundred feet the trail splits and if you go right will come to a power line road which makes for nice, secluded walking. Straight will follow the Peconic but dies out a bit. It is a nice walk if you live nearby.

Suffolk Hills County Park located east of Speonk-Riverhead Road is quite big with a lot of trails and undeveloped woods. Part of the park was burned in the 1995 Sunrise Fire but is growing back vigorously which is the beauty of the Pine Barrens. There are several straight trails made by bulldozers long ago that you can take to access "The Summit" where you can get nIce views of the surrounding land.

Cordwood Landing County Park which is in Miller Place is a small park that I would only recommend if you are in the area. It is on Landing Road on the east side with a paved pull-in. You then park in a dirt parking lot and head into the woods on a fairly wide path. The trail takes you to the Long Island Sound which is a great spot for fishing.

Located in Noyak is a small park called **Trout Pond Park** with a trail that surrounds the fairly big pond. Part of the trail is paved or on boardwalk and the rest is on dirt. This wonderful little pond filled with numerous trout and located on the south side of Noyac Road makes for a nice place to stroll. The path eventually hooks up with other trails that can take you for miles.

Hallock State Park, located on the north fork, is a great place to stop at after sightseeing in the summer or pumpkin picking in the fall. The park recently opened with a new visitor center, parking lot, and entrance. You can hike trails that pass Hallock Pond or go and view the Long Island Sound with a short walk.

Orient Beach State Park is located on the north fork at Orient Point and has 363 acres. The park has 45,000 feet of waterfront along with a maritime forest of red cedar, black-jack oak trees, and prickly-pear cactus. It was designated as one of NY's 28 National Natural Landmarks in 1980. The park is also a great spot for canoeing or kayaking.

Hubbard County Park is actually very big with its 1,815 acres but is quite limited with trails. It has two main trails with one located on Flanders Road and the other on Red Creek Road. There are both wide woods roads that start off in Pine Barrens habitat, which has been burned by a fire long ago and transition into saltwater marshes. The marshes are very nice especially in the spring and summer months. On these trails you will also come upon a Ducks Unlimited hunting lodge that is fairly active in the hunting season. To the east of Red Creek Road is a network of trails that pass by Penny Pond which has excellent freshwater fishing. The Paumanok Path runs through the park but is extremely overgrown.

Caumsett State Park is a 1,520 acre park located in Lloyd Harbor on the north shore. It is composed of many fields but also has a lot of forest habitat. There are over 200 different species of birds seen here making it an excellent place for bird watchers. The park also has a freshwater pond, saltwater marshes, and miles of coastline on the Long Island Sound. Nearby are several other preserves worth checking out, they are Target Rock National Wildlife Refuge, Trail View State Park, and Cold Spring Harbor State Park.

Farmingville Hills County Park is located on the north side of Horseblock Road in Farmingville. At the park the historical society runs an annual 5k on November 25 to raise money for repairs to the Bald Hill Schoolhouse located nearby. There is a 1.2 mile loop trail that is nice in the midst of the hustle and bustle of Farmingville. The parking lot is dirt but big and is located in a nice kept field along with a trail map.

Lily Pond County Park is located on Smithtown Boulevard just north of Lake Ronkonkoma. It borders nearby Commerdinger County Park which is the site of a historic homestead. The park is very small but is an excellent place for stunning views of Lily Pond which as the name implies is covered by Lily Pads.

Amsterdam Beach State Park Preserve is a preserve located in Montauk that opened in 2005 and has 199 acres. It is a quite nice park that is highly recommended but doesn't compare to the others in the area. There is a network of trails present with some going to the amazing views of the Atlantic Ocean. The park is composed of mainly small shrubs and no trees.

Edgewood Oak Brush Plains Preserve is located in Deer Park and has 813 acres that was originally supposed to be a psychiatric hospital. The preserve is dominated by pitch pine and scrub oak which are smaller trees compared to the towering pines of the rest of the island. At the park are extensive walking trails, bike trails, and a model airplane flying field. The park is a nice oasis in the midst of western Long Island.

Another park of interest is the **Long Pond Greenbelt** located near Sag Harbor. There are a ton of trails roaming through the woods passing several ponds such as Long Pond, Little Long Pond, Round Pond, and Crooked Pond. Long Pond, which is the biggest, is a spectacular pond comparable to Stump Pond in Blydenburgh County Park. This would have been an excellent park, maybe four or five on the list, but the only problem is the trails are not maintained. They are mostly overgrown and full of ticks except for one or two. With the proper management this park could have been much more than it currently is.

The last other park of interest is **Gardiner County Park** located on the south shore of the island in

Bayshore. It was originally owned by the Gardiner family which was Suffolk's first non-native land owners. The family still owns Gardiners Island out east which is one of the larger privately owned islands. The park is 231 acres and goes from a forest transitioning to marshes.

Credits

Paumanok Path Map p.15 from http://d-maps.com/carte.php?num_car=39843&lang=en

Connetquot River State Park trail map p.34 made by New York State Parks

Quogue Wildlife Refuge trail map p.38 photo by http://www.aaqeastend.com

Wertheim National Wildlife Refuge trail map p.47 made by Wertheim National Wildlife Refuge

Bald Hill County Park photo p.54 by PineyPhotosLI on Panaramio (Google Earth)

Manorville Hills County Park trail map p.61 made by David Warring copyright 2011

Mashomack Preserve trail map p.72 made by the Nature Conservancy

Mashomack Preserve photo p.74 took by Ed Sambolin from the Nature Conservancy Website

Rocky Point State Pine Barrens Preserve trail map p.87 made by the DEC

Wildwood State Park picture p.106 took by Trip Advisor

Robert Cushman Murphy County Park picture p.117 took by Mike R. Ebert from A Mike Who Likes to Hike blog

Camp Hero State Park map p.139 made by the New York State Parks Department

All other pictures not mentioned here is the sole property of the author, James Daniels, who retains all rights to the images. The images cannot be reproduced without permission of the author.

About The Author

James Daniels, middle schooler, is an avid hiker visiting various parks and preserves on Long Island and elsewhere. Accompanied by his dog, Candee, (who also loves to hike) he has visited almost all of the parks on Long Island. His love for the outdoors has fueled him to write *The Must See Hiking Destinations on Long Island.* A special thanks to my parents for taking me from Montauk to Nassau County to get the information necessary for this book. Stay tuned for my next book about my other interest, weather, coming soon.

SUFIS AND MYSTICS OF THE WORLD

FARZANA MOON

To Nandi, dearest of friends and wedding planner for our daughter Samina.

FOREWORD

Love is the theme of this book. To speak about love through the lips of the Sufis is like singing a song which warms and delights the hearts of all with its music of unity and wisdom. The word, Sufi, has countless definitions, but the simplest one is just one word, LOVE. And the path to Love is called Sufism. Sufi is the name first adopted by the devotees of Prophet Muhammad based on his own message of Love and Unity. Though intricately woven into the tapestry of Islam, Sufism is timeless and define-less, free of the limitations of creed or religion. Anyone can be a Sufi who wishes to seek God, or Beloved, inside the heart of mankind through the fire of love. Filling one's heart with so much love that there is no room left for hatred for anybody or anything! By cultivating such a character of Divine love, the Sufi as the paragon of a Lover is united with God, or Beloved, becoming the vessel of inspiration to share his or her message of unity in multiplicity. Many poets, sages, and philosophers have emerged since the seventh century onward as Sufis, also called the Masters. Rumi, Hafiz and Al-Hallaj are getting popular, just to name a few of the Sufi poets. The earliest known Sufis came mainly from Iraq, Iran, Egypt, Persia, Lebanon, and Afghanistan, but now they are found in all parts of the world. Sufis and Mystics of the world in this selection take us on a Journey toward the Throne of the Beloved. While love and longing are their oars of contemplation, their ship is the Heart of Mankind with sails billowing toward the heavens for Mystical Union. These pages of the book would take us on this voyage of Love and Ecstasy inside the hearts of the Sufis and the Mystics.

CHAPTER ONE

Hafiz
Born in Shiraz, in South-central Iran
Approximately between 1320-1389

I thought of You so often
That I completely became You
Little by little You drew near
And slowly but slowly I passed away
Javad Nurbakhsh

The symbol of the Sufis is a heart with wings.
In Sufi terminology, wine is Love, and tavern is Heart.
The simple definition of Sufi is, Love.
Sufis say, cultivate so much love in your heart that there is no room left for hatred.
Sufism is the Creed of the Heart, seeking God in the heart of mankind.
Sufism is the selfless experiencing and actualization of Truth.
Hafiz was the most beloved of poets in Persia, who lived around the same time as Chaucer in England, about one hundred year later after the famous Sufi poet, Rumi. Hafiz's real name was Shams-ud-din Muhammad. He adopted the pen name of Hafiz when he started writing poetry, and after he memorized the whole Quran by heart. *Hafiz literally means a person who has memorized the whole Quran by heart.* He was the son of a coal merchant, who died when Hafiz was in his teens. To support his two brothers and mother, he worked in a bakery, as well as studied theology. He had a natural gift for poetry, and became famous with his Gift of Writing in his twenties. While working at the bakery, he fell in love with a young woman of incredible beauty, whom he could not marry, and who became his Muse for Life. He did get married to someone else and had one child. He became a court poet, fell out of favor, fled Shiraz, and then was later reinstated to his post at the college. During those turbulent times, he met a famous Sufi poet of Shiraz by the

name of Attar (not the Attar of Nishapur), and became his disciple. From his twenties until the age of his death, Hafiz remained the disciple of Attar. But he was dissatisfied with his Master, and when he turned sixty, he confronted Attar with reproaches both loud and bitter.

Look at me! I am old, my wife and son are long dead. What I have gained by being your obedient disciple for all these years?

Be patient and one day you will know. Attar had replied gently.

I knew I would get that answer from you. Hafiz had fled in a fit of spiritual desperation.

Beginning that day, he began a forty day vigil. Drawing a circle on the ground, he sat within it for forty days and nights, without leaving it for food, drink, or even to relieve himself. On the fortieth day, the angel appeared to him, asking what he desired. Hafiz realized that during those forty days all his desires had disappeared. So he replied that his only wish was to serve his Master. Then he went to Attar's house, who was waiting for him at the door. They embraced, and then Attar gave him a special cup of aged wine. As they drank together, the intoxicating joy of wine opened his heart and dissolved every trace of separateness. With a laughter bubbling inside him like a fountain of *light*, Hafiz was forever drowned in love and united with God, his divine Beloved.

Sufism in the words of Carl W. Ernst:

Sufism is entry into exemplary behavior and departure from unworthy behavior.

Sufism means that God makes you die to yourself and makes you live in him.

The Sufi is single in essence; nothing changes him, nor does he change anything.

The sign of a sincere Sufi is that he feels poor when he has wealth, is humble when he has power, and is hidden when he has fame.

Sufism means that you own nothing and are owned by nothing.

Sufism means entrusting the soul to God most high for whatever He wishes.

Sufism means seizing spiritual realities and giving up on what creatures possess.

Sufism means kneeling at the door of the beloved, even if he turns you away.

Sufism is a state in which the conditions of humanity disappear.

Sufism is a blazing lightning bolt.

Prophet Muhammad said: *Love is the alphabet of the Sufis (mystics). They are humble, believe in Oneness, know the Voice of Silence, and are ego-less.*

I am He and He is I, except that I am he who I am and He is He who He is.
Prophet Muhammad
The divine path rejects no religion.
The essence of worship is to love.

A Lover's Tale by Ibn Al-Arabi

One day, one of God's lovers goes to the home of his Master. The Master begins to speak to him about love. Little by little, as the Master speaks, the lover begins to melt, becoming more and more subtle until he just flows like a trickling stream. His whole physical being dissolved in front of the Master, until there is nothing left but some water on the floor. Just then a friend of the Master enters the room and asks.

Where is that fellow who just arrived?

The Master points to the floor and says,

That man is that water.

That kind of melting was an astonishing transformation of the state. The man lost his density in such a way that he became what he originally was: a drop of liquid. Originally he had arrived at human *Form* from water, as God has said: *We created all life from water.*

This lover merely returned to his original essence, the water that is the source of life. And so we may draw the following conclusion: A lover is that being by whom everything is brought to life.

Here is an account of gods by Idries Shah:

This sense of the unity of inner, experiential, or symbolic religion was undoubtedly at work in the days when the peoples of the ancient world equated each others' gods one with the other. Mercury with Hermes and Hermes with Thoth is another example. It is this theosophical theory which the Sufis considered to be their own tradition, though not limited to the religious domain. Hence, as the Sufi has it:

I am in the pagan; I worship at the altar of the Jew; I am the idol of the Yemenite, the actual temple of the fire worshiper; the priest of the Magian; the inner reality of the cross-legged Brahmin meditating; the brush and the color of the artist; the suppressed, powerful personality of the scoffer. One does not supersede the other when a flame is thrown into another flame, they join at the point of *flamelessness.* You throw a torch at a candle, and then say, *See, I have annihilated the candle's flame.* (Ishan Kaiser in Speech of the Sages.)

Be you perfect as your Father in Heaven is Perfect. Jesus

The title poem by Javad Nurbakhsh is the essence of Sufism. He was born in Kerman, Iran. He attended the University of Tehran, and received his medical diploma in 1952. He was initiated into the Nimatullahi Sufi Path at the age of sixteen.

Sufi and Sufism:

The root word Sufi in Greek means Wisdom, and in Arabic, Purity.

Sufism derives its name from the Greek word *Sophia,* which means Wisdom, and from the Arabic word Suf — wool, meaning Purity. It refers to the pure white woolen garments worn by certain Sufis.

Sufi is a person who has attained union with his/her Beloved through the Fire of Love.

The name Sufi was first adopted by the devotees of Prophet Muhammad from his message of Unity. Adopting a mystical tradition of Islam known as Sufism!

Sufi is a mystic who is closer to God, and is the Friend of God. Sufis are the mystics who like to see God while living. For Sufi mystics, it is necessary to understand mysticism.

Mysticism is the essence of all knowledge which is obvious neither to refinement, nor to receptivity of faculties with the super-conscious mind. So Mystery of the Mysterious is experienced through enlightenment.

Enlightenment is perceived in darkness and bewilderment by the grace of God. Then one sees the Light, and Ignorance melts away.

Sufi poetry is the child of both mystery and enlightenment. It is born from the Union of Love, and draws towards its Source with absolute devotion without the least care of reward or rejection from the Beloved

Source, thus succeeding in unfolding the Beauty of Love in sheer joy of bliss and ecstasy.

Sufi does not speak to God, but from God, seeing Truth in all Forms. A Sufi's consciousness is shifted from personal point of view to Divine point of view. Looking at everything from two points of view! From his/her own, and from that of Another.

Sufism is the cultivation of Divine character through Love. It is not a philosophy, in that it is based on nature of Reality which is transcendent. All philosophical systems are necessarily closed since no mental form can encompass the Infinite. It is only the Spiritual Heart, the instrument of intuition, which is above forms and capable of holding the Throne of God.

HAFIZ—the Heart of Sufi Poetry

The voice of the river that has emptied into the Ocean
Now laughs and sings just like God

All I know is love
And I find my heart Infinite
And Everywhere
All is written within the mind
To help and instruct the dervish
In dance and romance and prayer
We offer love to everyone
And in love accept all blame
For in our Way, to be offended
Is faithlessness to God

I hear the voice
Of every creature and plant
Every world and sun and galaxy
Singing the Beloved's Name!

A poet is someone
Who can pour light into a cap

Then raise it to nourish
Your beautiful parched, holy mouth

The dark night, the fear of waves
The terrifying whirlpool
How can they know of our state
Those who go lightly along the shore

Write a thousand luminous secrets
Upon the wall of existence
So that even a blind man will know
Where we are
And join us in this love

What is this precious love and laughter
Budding in our hearts
It is the glorious sound
Of a soul waking up

I am in love with every church and mosque and temple
And any kind of shrine
Because I know it is there
That people say the different names
Of the one God

God Just Came Near
No
One
In need of love
Can sit with my verse for
An hour
And then walk away without carrying
Golden tools
And feeling that God
Just came
Near

I Have Learned So Much
I
Have
Learned
So much from God
That I can no longer
Call
Myself
A Christian, a Hindu, a Muslim
A Buddhist, a Jew
The Truth has shared so much of Itself
With me
That I can no longer call myself
A man, a woman, an angel
Or even pure
Soul
Love has
Befriended Hafiz so completely
It has turned to ash
And freed
Me
Of every concept and image
My mind has ever known

It Felt Love
How
Did the rose
Ever open its heart
And give to this world
All its
Beauty
It felt the encouragement of light
Against its
Being
Otherwise

We all remain
Too
Frightened

The Ambience of Love
We all
Sit in His orchestra
Some play their
Fiddles
Some wield their
Clubs
Tonight is worthy of music
Let's get loose
With
Compassion
Let's drown in the delicious
Ambience of
Love

Why Aren't We Screaming Drunks
The sun once glimpsed God's true nature
And has never been the same
Thus that radiant sphere
Constantly pours its energy
Upon this earth
And does He from behind
The veil
With a wonderful God like that
Why isn't everyone a screaming drunk
Hafiz's guess is this:
Any thought that you are better or less
Than another man
Quickly
Breaks the wine
Glass

The Heart's Coronation
The pawn
Always sits stunned
Chained, unable to move
Beneath God's magnificent power
It is essential for the heart's coronation
For the pawn to realize
There is nothing but divine movement
In this
World

Stop Being So Religious
What
Do sad people have in
Common
It seems
They have built a shrine
To the past
And often go there
And do a strange wail and
Worship
What is the beginning of
Happiness
Is to stop being
So religious
Like
That

Get The Blame Straight
Understanding the physics of God
His Indivisible Nature
Makes every universe and atom confess:
I am just a helpless puppet that cannot dance
Without the movement of His hand
Dear ones
This curriculum tonight is for the advanced

And will
Get all the blame straight
End the mental
Lawsuits
That
Clog
The Brain

A Shift in the Breeze
For a long time
I have done tavern-work
Wearing the clothes
Of emptiness, singing
With those who feel joy
But I didn't catch the subtle
Truth-fragrance there
So I am leaving
Leaving the sweet partridge
Of the Beloved along
Hoping to be ambushed
I walk the open street
Like a breeze
In which the basil and the rose
Rise and fall in prayer
I am trying to entice
The arrow, your glance
The threshold-kiss of Majesty
To land there
This is what I do:
In a conventionally religious
Assembly, *I am Hafiz*
Who knows the entire
Quran by heart
While in a tavern
I am the dreg-drinker
Notice the dazzling turn

Of that change

The Taste of my Poison
Don't ask me to describe
The taste of my poison
At the end of years wandering
I have chosen a Friend
Don't ask who!
I weep in the doorway
Last night I heard you saying
What cannot be said
Now you motion to me
Don't tell
The pain of my being in the room
Alone is really what
Cannot be spoken
So, like Hafiz
I walk the love-road
Aware in a way
That has no name

Sometimes I say to a poem
Not now,
Can't you see I am bathing!
But the poem usually doesn't care
And quips
Too bad, Hafiz
No getting lazy—
You promised God you would help out
And He just came up with this
New Tune
Sometimes I say to a poem
I don't have the strength
To wring out another drop
Of the Sun.

And the poem will often respond
By climbing into a barroom table
Then lifts its skirt, winks
Causing the whole sky to Fall

The Seed Cracked Open
It used to be
That when I would wake up in the morning
I could with confidence say
What I am going to do
That was before the seed
Cracked open
Now Hafiz is certain:
There are not two of us housed
In this body
During the shopping together in the market and
Tickling each other
While fixing the evening's food
Now when I awake
All the internal instruments play the same music:
God, what love-mischief can We do
For the world
Today

Tired of Speaking Sweetly
Love wants to reach out and manhandle us
Break all our teacup talk of God
If you had the courage and
Could give the Beloved His choice, some nights,
He would just drag you around the room
By your hair
Ripping from your grip all those toys in the world
That bring you no joy
Love sometimes gets tired of speaking sweetly
And wants to rip to shreds
All your erroneous notions of truth

That make you fight within yourself, dear one
And with others
Causing the world to weep
On too many fine days
God wants to manhandle us
Lock us inside of a tiny room with Himself
And practice His dropkick
The Beloved sometimes wants
To do us a great favor:
Holds us upside down
And shakes all the nonsense out
But when we hear
He is in such a *playful drunken mood*
Most everyone I know
Quickly packs their bags and hightails it
Out of town

In Need of the Breath
My heart
Is an unset jewel
Upon the tender night
Yearning for its dear old friend
The Moon
When the Nameless One debuts again
Ten thousand facets of my being unfurl wings
And reveal such radiance inside
I enter a realm divine —
I too begin to so sweetly cast light
Like a lamp
Through the streets of this
World
My heart is an unset jewel
Upon existence
Waiting for the Friend's touch
Tonight
My heart is an unset ruby

Offered bowed and weeping to the Sky
I am dying in these cold hours
For the resplendent glance of God
I am dying
Because of a divine remembrance
Of who—I really am
Hafiz, tonight
Your soul
Is a brilliant reed instrument
In need of the breath of the
Christ

Allah, Allah, Allah
Now
The sky-drum plays
All by itself in my head
Singing all day long
Allah, Allah,Allah

The Sun Never Says
Even
After
All this time
The Sun never says to the earth
You owe Me
Look
What happens
With a love like that
It lights the
Whole
Sky

CHAPTER TWO

JALALAL-DIN RUMI

Born in the city of Balkh (now in Afghanistan)
1207-1273

Step out of the circle of time
And into the circle of love

Rumi

Musical instruments of the Sufis: Flute, harp, rebab, reed pipe, tamboura, tambourine.

Sufi, Sufism and Sufi poetry is associated with music, dance and remembrance of God. And Sufis believe that if one wishes to be near God, one must seek God within the hearts of others. In other words, one must seek *light* much like the light of sunshine, where one can see the reflection of the same face in All. In Sufi tradition, *to bring joy to a single heart is better than to build many shrines for worship—*Robert Frager. *To enslave one soul by kindness is worth more than the setting free of a thousand slaves—*Prophet Muhammad.

Historically, Sufism dates as far back as to 2nd century BC. Initially, Arabic was used as a mystical expression in the form of poetry during the ninth century. Eleventh century brought forth the flowering of Persian poetry, sung by the mystics and the troubadours. Other languages, such as Hindi and Turkish cultivated the love for Sufi poetry, and it began to flourish, sprouting forth in many Sufi traditions which are still extant up to our present time.

Rumi started his own tradition of Love and Dance, which is becoming popular in the west as an art form of Unity and Universal wisdom. Rumi, though born in Balkh, spent most of his life in Konya (also known as Rum) in Turkey. The city of Balkh was invaded by the Mongols when Rumi was only twelve, and his family left for a pilgrimage to Mecca. On their way they stopped at Nishapur, and met the famous Sufi Attar. Rumi's father himself was a Sufi, claiming lineage from the great Sufi, Al Ghazali. While Attar talked with Rumi, he was so impressed that he told

Rumi's father that Rumi would soon be kindling a fire in all the world's lovers of God. And as they left, Attar sang his farewell, exclaiming: *Look, there goes a sea followed by an ocean!*

Rumi got married at the age of twenty-one, and a son was born to him after a couple of years. By that time, he was well versed in logic, theology, mathematics and astronomy. He worked as a professor in Konya, and people from all parts of the East came to him for advice and lecture. He was always reading and searching for something beyond words and expressions, but could never find that *Something. His heart always longing and restless, unable to express its own emptiness and Yearning.* He was in his forties when a revelation of *love* struck him like the bolt of lightning, transforming him from a man of learning to a man gone mad with love and ecstasy.

There are several tales which talk of this revelation as an awakening to love temporal, followed by love Divine, but one of them reflects his true state of joy and intoxication. One afternoon, Rumi was sitting in his college library, when a Sufi master by the name of Shams Tabrizi sailed in uninvited. Judging from his appearance to be a vagabond or some uncouth intruder, Rumi didn't even greet him. Shams Tabrizi, without introducing himself, let his gaze wander over the bookshelves, and asked.

What are these?

You wouldn't understand. Was Rumi's impatient response.

Shams Tabrizi stood still, fixing his gaze to one shelf in the corner. Suddenly, flames from out of nowhere started to leap upward from under the books.

What is this? Rumi cried in horror.

You wouldn't understand. Shams Tabrizi stalked out of the library.

Rumi sat there stunned for a moment. The flames had disappeared, and so had the sorcerer. But he leaped to his feet as if stung and raced after the man, whose words had cut through his *ignorance* like the blade of icy wisdom. Finding him on the street, he clung to him and prostrated himself at his feet. He was weeping; his heart was opened with the fire of love, humbled and transfigured, as if it had seen the face of Eternal Beloved. Thus began the journey, for Rumi, from love temporal to love Divine. Rumi became oblivious to the world, as he went to a retreat with

Shams Tabrizi for forty days. After he came out, he became the vessel of divine inspiration. Rumi's friendship with Shams Tabrizi in the role of Master and Disciple incited the jealousy of his students. Shams Tabrizi vanished all of a sudden, and the rumor was that Rumi's students murdered the Sufi saint. Rumi was grief-stricken, pouring forth his love and grief in verses sublime and profound. Then he began a Sufi school known as the, Mevlevi Order, the Order of Whirling Dervishes, in which music and dance was incorporated to attain Union with the Beloved.

Some scholars conjecture that this dance was taught to Rumi by Shams Tabrizi during the forty day Retreat. It's a beautiful dance, expressing the deepest secrets of mystical Love. The Sufis are dressed all in white, the symbolic gowns of eternal light, spinning around their axis to the notes of flute, and whirling around the center, as though the atoms are dancing around the Sun, which attracts them to set them in motion. They dance in intense spiritual concentration, with one hand outstretched towards the heaven to receive blessings and the other turned towards the earth to transmit them. They are enraptured in the remembrance of God, listening to the *call of God*. When this love for God strikes the heart of the Sufi, his inner being is moved. The spiritual music transforms him from himself to a state where he senses in his heart the awesome, all-absorbing presence of God.

But then scholars dig deep into the psyche of us all, attributing Sufism to the time of Creation. They say, Adam was the first Sufi, since God taught him the names of all creatures, including the beautiful Names of God. Tracing the Creation of the Universe, its development, its breakdown and destruction, and finally its joy! The music of our soul is the remembrance of God, symbolic of the sound of Creation. It is the sound of the falling of the leaves in the Garden of Eden, as the Sufis say.

To understand Rumi in this context, we listen to the songs of his joy, longing, separation from the Beloved, and finally the Bliss and Union in Love and Awakening. Annihilation and Resurrection! Fire and ecstasy! Rumi calls his Master in the drunken ecstasy of his poems, the Sun and the Beloved, through whose light he attained Divine Union.

A canal may itself not drink, but it performs the function of carrying water to the thirsty. Rumi

Famous Sufis in timeless Circle

Prophet Muhammad	570-632
Rabia	717-802
Al Hallaj	858-922
Firdausi	949-1020
Abu Said	978-1061
Omar Khayyam	1048-1123
Shams Tabrizi	1148-1247
Farid-ud-din Attar	1136-1230
Al Surhawardi	1151-1191
Ibn Al-Arabi	1165-1240
Ibn Al-Farid	1181-1235
Jalalal-Din-Rumi	1207-1273
Sa'adi	1207-1291
Hafiz	1320-1389
Jami	1439-1520
Kabir	1448-1518
St. John of the Cross	1542-1591
Sarmad	1590-1660

A journey from love temporal to Love Divine

Love is the alphabet of the Sufis. Through love is attained union with God. The pilgrimage of love for a Sufi is wild and ecstatic, first consumed by the human attributes of beauty and wisdom, and then annihilated by the fire of love in mystical union with the Beloved. Beloved is in the heart of all human beings. And a Sufi, who has inhaled the fragrance of love, steps out of the circle of love, falling into another Circle of Love.

The site of love is the heart, and the heart is pure gold, the pearl of the breast's ocean, the ruby of the inmost mystery's mine. The hand of no one else has touched it, and the eye of no one who is not a confidant has fallen upon it. The witnessing of God's Majesty has polished it, and the burnisher of the Unseen has placed its seal upon it, making it bright and limpid. Since the heart's work has all of this, the Presence of Exaltation has a love for it. He held the beauty of love before the hearts of the great ones, and the traces of the lights of unqualified love's beauty appeared in the mirror of their hearts. So, our love abides through His love, not His love through our love. (Sufi teaching by William C. Chittick).

RUMI

SOUL OF THE POET
Listen to the way the reed flute grieves
Telling stories of its separation

I was stripped of the body, he was stripped of illusion
Now I proudly stroll toward the final union

The lovers are a sect distinct
From all others
With a faith and creed all of their own

The creatures are set in motion by love
Love by God in all eternity
The wind dances because of the spheres
The trees because of the wind

Secrets fall from the Sufi's hands
Whole kingdoms for the taking
Unlike someone who begs on the street for bread
A dervish begs to give his life away

This human face is a shape
Tethered in the stall of pain
Part god, part angel, part beast
A secret charm, rarely released
We are the mirror as well as the face in it
We are drunk on this life of God
We are both the pain and its cure, we are
The fresh, cool water and the jar that pours

A Craftsman
Pulled a reed
From the reed-bed
Cut holes in it, and
Called it a human being
Since then, it's been wailing
A tender agony of parting
Never mentioning the skill
That gave it life as a flute

Humble living does not
Diminish, it fills
Going back to a simpler self
Gives wisdom
When a man makes up a story
For his child, he becomes
A father and a child
Together, listening

Leave, with you
Scholarship and
Your philosophies
Even if you reduced them
To a single hair's breath
There would be no room here
For those, as now
The dawn comes up
In the wholeness of the Sun
It is an impudence
To light lamps

If you could get rid
Of yourself just once
The secret of secrets
Would open to you

The face of the Unknown
Hidden beyond the universe
Would appear on the
Mirror of your perception

There is no salvation for the soul
But to fall in love
It has to creep and crawl
Among the lovers first
Only lovers can escape
From these Two Worlds
This was written in creation
Only from the Heart
Can you touch the sky
The rose of Glory
Can only be raised in the Heart

Our pure hearts roam across the world
We get bewildered by all the idols we see
Yet what we are trying to understand
In everything is what we already are

See how the hand is invisible while the pen is writing
The horse careening, yet the rider is unseen
The arrow flying, but the bow out of sight
Individual souls existing
While the Soul of the souls is hidden

The Beloved's water washes all illness away
The Beloved's rose garden of Union has no thorns
I've heard it said there's a window that opens
Between heart and heart
But if there are no walls
There's no need even for a window

The tart and hearty grapes, destined to ripe
Will at last become one in heart
By the breath of the masters of heart
They will grow steadily to grape-hood
Shedding duality and malice and strife
Till in maturity, they rend their skins
And become the mellow wine of Union

Thou didst contrive this *I* and *We* in order that
Thou mightest play the game of worship with Thyself
That all *I's and Thou's* should become one soul and
At last should be submerged in the Beloved

Oh heart, sit with someone
Who knows the heart
Go under the tree
Which has fresh blossoms

I've spent my life, my heart
And my eyes this way
I used to think that love
And beloved are different
I know now they are the same
I was seeing two in One

If there be any lover in the world, o Muslims, 'tis I
If there be any believer, or Christian hermit, 'tis I
This wine dregs, the cupbearer, the minstrel
The harp and the music
The beloved, the candle, the drink and the joy of the drunken—'tis I
The two-and-seventy creeds and sects in the world
Do not really exist: I swear by God that every creed and sect—'tis I
Earth and air and water and fire, nay, body and soul too—'tis I
Truth and falsehood, good and evil, ease and difficulty from first to
last
Knowledge and learning and asceticism and piety and faith—'tis I

The fire of Hell, be assured, with its flaming limbos
Yes, and Paradise and Eden and the Houris—'tis I
This earth and heaven with all they hold
Angels, Peris, Genies and Mankind—'tis I

I am drunk with love
Neither now here, nor nowhere
I am incapable of anything
But celebration
The mystics speak in a hundred different ways
But if God is one and the Way is one, how could
Their meaning be other than One, what appears
In different disguises is one essence
But a unity of substance

If you are for real
Risk everything for love
If not, get out of here
Half a heart isn't enough
You keep setting out to find God
But end up spending more time
In rundown wayside taverns

I drank it down in one
And collapsed intoxicated by purity
Ever since I can't tell if I exist or not
Sometimes I know the bliss
Of the *I* that looks through my eyes
Other time my habits dump me back in the offal
But then there it is—that aroma once again
I am returned to the Rose Garden

One went to the door of the Beloved and
Knocked, a voice asked, *who is there*
He answered, *it is I*
The voice said, *There is no room for Me and Thee*

The door was shut
After a year of solitude and deprivation he returned and
Knocked, a voice from within asked, *who is there*
The man said, *It is Thee*
The door was opened for him

We have become drunk and our heart has departed
It has fled from us—wither it has gone
When it saw that the chain of reason was broken
Immediately, my heart took to flight
It will not have gone to any other place
It has departed to seclusion of God
Seek it not in the house, for it is of the air
It is a bird of the air, and has gone into the air
It is the white falcon of the Emperor, it has taken flight
And departed to the Emperor

My verse resembles the bread of Egypt
Night passes over it, and you cannot eat it any more
Devour it the moment it is fresh
Before the dust settles upon it
Its place is the warm climate of heart
In this world it dies of cold
Like a fish it quivered for an instant on dry land
Another moment and you see it cold
Even if you eat it imagining it is fresh
It is necessary to conjure up many images
When you drink, it is really your own imagination
It is no old tale, my good man

Hearken to this Reed forlorn
Breathing even since 'twas torn
From its rushy bed
A strain of impassioned love and pain
The secret of my song, though near
None can see and none can hear

Oh, for a friend to know the sign
And mingle all his soul with mine
'Tis the flame of Love fired me
'Tis the wine of love inspired me
Wouldst thou know how lovers bleed
Hearken, hearken to the Reed

Once you have been filled with the Wine Everlasting
You will not see the goblet, just smell its perfume
All inanimate things will give you their greetings
And tell you their secrets, like friends and relatives
Once the Spirit Supreme has embraced you in Love
All forms turn to spirits before your eyes
The time has come for me to dance in a circle
With face unveiled, Love is singing love-poems
Like the reed rose, Love goes out for a ride
All the sweet herbs follow behind, like troops
Bring sweetmeats and wine and sit before me
You whose face is a candle, whose wine is like fire

Last night I saw *poverty* in a dream
I became beside myself from its beauty
From the loveliness and perfection of the grace of poverty
I was dumbfounded until dawn
I saw poverty like a mine of ruby
So that through its hue I became clothed in silk
I heard the clamorous rapture of lovers
I heard the cry of *drink now, drink*
I saw a ring all drunken with poverty
I saw its ring in my own ear
From the midst of my soul a hundred surgings rose
When I beheld the surging of the sea
Heaven uttered a hundred cries
I am the slave of such a leader

Whitewater carries me along
I am a millstone
Turning day and night
Moaning and creaking
By my turning, you know
The power and motion
Of the invisible river
The beloved friend is a river
The night-sky is a water-wheel
Revolving in that
The love-river doesn't rest
In it, if you grab a branch
The river breaks it
Any attachment you have
Take hold strongly and
Let it be snapped off
If you don't see the huge
Sky-turnings, look at the
Broken sticks moving by, and
The foam-bubbles around you

If a tree could move on foot or wing
It would not suffer the pain of the saw or the blows of the axe
And if the sun did not travel on wing and foot all night
How would the world be illumined at morning-tide
If the salt water did not rise from the sea to the sky
Whence would the garden be revived by rain and torrent
When the drop departed from its homeland and returned
It encountered a shell and became a pearl
Did not Joseph go from his father on a journey, weeping
Did he not on the journey attain felicity and victory and kingdom
Did not Mustafa go on a journey toward Yathrib, gain sovereignty
And become king of a hundred lands
And you—if you have no foot, choose to journey into yourself
Like a ruby mine, be receptive to the print from the sunbeams

Make a journey out of self into self, my master
For by such a journey earth became a mine of gold
Go out of sourness and bitterness towards sweetness
Just as a thousand sorts of fruits have escaped out of bitterness
Seek sweetness from the Sun, the Pride of Tabriz
For every fruit gains comeliness from the light of the Sun

Come, for today is for us a day of festival
Henceforth joy and pleasure are on increase
Clap hands, say, *Today is all happiness*
From the beginning it was manifestly a fine day
Who is there in this world like our Friend
Who has seen such a festival in hundred years
Earth and heaven are filled with sugar
In every direction sugarcane has sprouted
The roar of the pearl-scattering sea has arrived
The world is full of waves, the sea is invisible
Muhammad has returned from the Ascension
Jesus has arrived from the fourth Heaven
Every coin which is not of this place is counterfeit
Every wine which is not the cup of the Soul is impure
What a splendid assembly where the saki is good fortune
And his companions are Junaid and Bayazid
Crop-sickness afflicted me when I was desirous
I did not know that God Himself desires us
Now I have fallen asleep and stretched out my feet
Since I have realized that good fortune has drawn me on

I died from the mineral kingdom and became a plant
I died to vegetable nature and became an animal
I died to animality and became a human being
Next time I will die to human nature
And lift up my head among the angels
Once again I will leave the angelic nature
And become that which you cannot imagine

Those who don't feel this love
Pulling them like a river
Those who don't drink dawn
Like a cup of spring water
Or take in sunset like supper
Those who don't want to change
Let them sleep
This love is beyond the study of theology
That old trickery and hypocrisy
If you want to improve your mind that way
Sleep on
I have given up on my brain
I have torn the cloth to shreds
And thrown it away
If you are not completely naked
Wrap your beautiful robe of words
Around you
And sleep

I adore not the Cross nor the Crescent, I am not a Gerber, nor a Jew
East nor West, land nor sea is my home, I have kin not with angel or gnome
I am wrought not of fire nor of foam, I am shaped not of dust nor of dew
I was born not in China afar, not in Saqsin and not in Bulghar
Not in India where five rivers are, nor Iraq nor Khorasan I grew
Not in this world nor that world I dwell, not in Paradise, neither in Hell
Not from Eden and Rizwan I fell, not from Adam my lineage I drew
My place is the placeless, my trace is the traceless
'Tis neither body nor soul, for I belong to the soul of the Beloved
I have put duality away, I have seen that the two worlds are one
One I seek, one I know, one I see, one I call

For my funeral
Call the drummers, timbal beaters and tambourine players
March toward my grave dancing thus
Happy, gay, intoxicated, with hands clapping
So that people would know that the friends of God
Go happy and smiling toward the place of meeting

CHAPTER THREE

OMAR KHAYYAM

Born at Nishapur in Khorasan (Iran)
1048-1123
Blasphemy and religion, Kaaba
And pagan temple
For the true lover, are one and the same
A Sufi saying

Sufi poetic analogy—Grape denotes interior experience.

Sufis wear the cloak of *love* patched with many colors, but the color dyeing all those robes in the purity of whiteness is the Color of Longing for the Beloved. Their quest is to lose themselves in love and to seek the Bliss of Union. Their deep love for humanity liberates them from the shackles of dogma and hypocrisy. Once, inspired, either they drown themselves in the baptismal fountain of Love with the Beloved, or emerge forth Purified, sharing their wisdom with the world in a way the world deigns to understand.

Omar Khayyam was in the categories of *Sufis Purified,* flinging his genius to the winds, and speaking with the sages and fools of his time in a tongue which they could understand. *Khayyam means tent-maker,* this Sufi poet named as Hakim Omar at his birth, adopted the pen name Khayyam later, since he practiced the trade of tent-making in his youth. He studied at a college in Nishapur under the tutelage of Imam Mowaffak. Philosophy and theology were his areas of interest, but his studies didn't end there, he became proficient in science, mathematics and astronomy during the later years of his life. His heart always passionate for truth and justice lured him toward Sufic Thought, if not toward Sufic Traditions. In his time, Islam was in great throes of lies and distortion, which had started right after the death of Prophet Muhammad, but now the pangs of such suffering were reaching the heights of bigotry and hypocrisy. So, after years of contemplation and attaining a glimpse of his Beloved, he began a crusade to unveil the false piety of the so-called Sufis and claimants of truth, earning their hatred in recompense to his own *light* of love and wisdom.

Omar Khayyam is remembered as the *King of Wisdom.* During his college years, he met two young men of his taste who became his intimate friends. Hassan Sabbah and Nizam ul Mulk are the names of these friends who became the students of Omar Khayyam's illustrious teacher, Imam Mowaffak. This teacher was revered by all, engendering a strong belief that all his students would attain the height of great fame and fortune. Without exception, this trio of friends believed in this general belief, and were in the habit of discussing their future with the wand of hope and imagination! One day, after the lecture, when they were tearing this *belief* into shreds with their arguments, Hassan Sabbah exclaimed suddenly.

Don't we all agree that the pupils of Imam Mowaffak will attain to fortune? Now, even if we all do not attain thereto, without doubt, one of us will. What then shall be our mutual bond and pledge? Hassan's eyes were lit up with mirth and anticipation.

What do you propose? Omar Khayyam had asked.

We would agree to whatever you say. Nizam ul Mulk was quick to consent, even on Omar Khayyam's behalf.

Well, let us make a vow, that to whomsoever this fortune falls, he shall share it equally with the rest, and reserve no pre-eminence for himself. Hassan Sabbah proposed.

So, the three friends shook hands on this pledge, and cultivated deeper friendship during their stay at college. After graduation, they went their separate ways, and didn't see each other for years. Nizam ul Mulk traveled from Khorasan to TransOxiana, then wandered from Kabul to Ghazni. When he returned to Nishapur, he was invested with the high rank of administrator to the Sultanate of Sultan Alp Arslan. Meanwhile, Omar Khayyam had immersed himself deep into the studies of science and astronomy, supporting himself by working with a tent-maker. Hassan Sabbah had disappeared, reappearing suddenly as soon as Nizam ul Mulk became a vizier to the Sultan. Carrying the old pledge under his sleeves, Hassan Sabbah demanded a post in the government. Nizam ul Mulk succeeded in attaining this post for his friend, since he had become a favorite of the Sultan. Omar Khayyam, on the other hand, appealed to his friend, but his appeal-request was unusual. All he wanted was that Nizam ul Mulk let him live in a corner under the shadow of his fortunes, so that he could spread wide the advantages of Science and pray for the long life and prosperity of his friend. His request was most willingly granted.

Hassan Sabbah turned out to be a rebel and plotter. After attaining high post in the government by the generosity of his friend, he plunged himself into a maze of intrigues. He was apprehended by the Sultan himself, and forced to leave his post in disgrace. Later, he became the head of Persian sect of the Ismailians. Joined a band of crusaders, and amongst the countless victims of his assassin's dagger were his old friend, Nizam ul Mulk himself.

Omar Khayyam, who had been granted a pension of twelve hundred mithkals of gold by Nizam ul Mulk, employed his time and talent to the benefit of the people and government. Under the Sulatanate of Malik Shah, he went to Merv, and obtained great praise for his proficiency in Science. When Malik Shah was determined to reform the calendar, Omar Khayyam was one of his eight learned men employed to this task. This calendar was known as Jalali calendar.

Omar Khayyam also devised astronomical tables, and taught at a college in Nishapur. Contemplating all his life about hell and heaven, along with science and astronomy, he became a Sufi by his inner need and longing, and a poet by necessity to enlighten his people against the evil of false piety, pride and hypocrisy. Thus earning hatred from his countrymen, though winning the love of his students who remained devoted to him heart and soul! One of them, recalling with affection and sadness after the death of the King of Wisdom, this snippet of a conversation. One student was walking in the garden with Omar Khayyam, when Omar Khayyam stopped under one tree and said, *My tomb shall be in a spot where the north wind may scatter roses over it.*

Years later, when that student visited the tomb of his revered Master, he was awestruck by the prophetic words of Omar Khayyam. There was this tomb outside a garden in Nishapur, and trees laden with fruit stretched their boughs over the garden wall, scattering their flowers over the grave, even the tombstone was hidden under their white petals.

Omar Khayyam's Rubaiyat, were not known in the west until translated by Edward Fitzgerald, an English poet who lived between Year 1809 to Year 1883.

Sufism is a way of Love, a way of Devotion, a way of Knowledge.

There are several Sufi Orders with their own teaching of discipline and initiation, but four major ones are as follows:

Qadiri Order: This Order was started by Abdul Qadir Geylani who was born in the city of Jilan in Persia, 1077-1166. He lived and studied in Baghdad under the spiritual guidance of Shaykh Hammad. His teachings were simple and practical. He taught by example, stressing the need of love for all, and Remembrance that God is everywhere! One day to test his disciples, he gave them one chicken each, ordering them to slaughter the chickens where no one can see them. Next day, all the disciples (with the exception of one) returned with their chickens slaughtered, explaining their secrecy as to no one seeing them. Some had accomplished this task inside a dark room; some had gone to the jungle, some to the riverside. The last disciple came all dejected, hiding his chicken inside the folds of his robe.

I couldn't execute your order, Master. The disciple lamented. *I tried to find a place where no one would see me. But wherever I went, I felt the presence of God watching me, so how could I slaughter this chicken?*

Of course, the disciple was chosen as his successor.

Chishti Order: Khwaja Muinuddin Chishti was born in Sistan in East Persia, 1138-1236. He was tutored by a great Sufi of his time, Khwaja Sahib. They both went on a pilgrimage to Mecca and Medina. In Medina, Muinuddin Chishti saw Prophet Muhammed in his dream, instructing him to take the message of love, unity and brotherhood to India. He left Medina, passing through Herat, Isfahan, Bokhara, Lahore and Delhi, meeting Sufis and sages on the way. Finally, he reached Rajaputna, and settled in Ajmer. Both Hindus and Muslims became his sincere devotees, and after his death built a shrine at Ajmer, which is still visited by millions throughout the year.

Mevlevi Order: This Order was started by Rumi after the death of his beloved Master, Shams Tabrizi. Later known as Dancing with gods, or Whirling dervishes! The dancing is a reference to the circling of the spirit around the cycle of existing things on account of receiving the effects of the unveiling and revelations; and this is the state of the mystic. The whirling is a reference to the spirit's standing with God in its secret. The leaping up is a reference to his being drawn from the human station to the station of the Union.

Naqahbandi Order: This Sufi Order takes its name from a Master by the name of Naqshis, born in Turkey, 1318-1389. Their Sufic discipline, in conformity with Sufism is, Love and Unity. God created both worlds for man. He created man for his ability to know God. The basis of their discipline is Islam, and they have further split in other Sufi Orders.

If Love is the alphabet of the Sufis, Wisdom is their book of Knowledge. This knowledge is attained from within in some sort of daze and intoxication. While quaffing the wine of spiritual union, some of them return to the world as the vessels of wisdom, veiling their wisdom in clouds of inspiration, yet throwing open the doors of both the worlds for us to explore and contemplate. If one could see Seekers as the victims of mystical infatuations with visions of reality, not the truth, then one could define sensual pleasures as the representations of a deeper joy, also devoid of truth. To a Sufi, Truth is One and Truth is Love, wearing a cloak of doubt and yearning until completely annihilated.

OMAR KHAYYAM

THE SUFI-ASTRONOMER OF PERSIA
Ah, Love! Could you and I with him conspire
To grasp this sorry Scheme of Things entire
Would we not shatter it to bits—and then
Re-mold it nearer to the Heart's Desire

Some in deep thought spirit seek
Some lost in awe, of doubt reek
I fear the voice, hidden but not weak
Cry out *Awake! Both ways are oblique*

Indeed the idols I have loved so long
Have done my credit in this World much wrong
Have drowned my Glory in a shallow cup
And sold my Reputation for a song

Before the phantom of False morning died
Methought a voice within the Tavern cried
When all the Temple is prepared within
Why nods the drowsy worshipper outside

Ah, my Beloved fill the Cup that clears
Today of Past Regrets and Future Fears
Tomorrow—why, Tomorrow I may be
Myself with Yesterday's Seven Thousand Years

There was a door to which I found no Key
There was the Veil through which I might not see
Some little talk awhile of Me and Thee
There was—and then no more of Thee and Me

Perplex no more with Human or Divine
Tomorrow's tangle to the winds resign
And lose your fingers in the tresses of
The Cypress—slender Minister of Wine

When You and I behind the Veil are past
Oh, but the long, long while the World shall last
Which of our Coming and Departure heeds
As the Sea's self should heed a pebble-cast

You know, my Friends, with what a brave Carouse
I made a Second Marriage in my house
Divorced old barren Reason from my Bed
And took the Daughter of the Vine to Spouse

The Grape that can with Logic absolute
The Two-and-Seventy jarring Sects confute
The sovereign alchemist that in a trice
Life's leaden metal into Gold transmute

Oh, threats of Hell and Hopes of Paradise
One thing at least is certain—This Life flies
One thing is certain and the rest is Lies
The flower that once has bloomed for ever dies

I sent my Soul through the Invisible
Some letter of that After-life to spell
And by and by my Soul returned to me
And answered, *I Myself am Heaven and Hell*

Now the New Year reviving old Desires
The thoughtful Soul to Solitude retires
Where the White Hand of Moses on the Bough
Puts out, and Jesus from the ground suspires

Come, fill the Cup, and in the fire of Spring
Your Winter-garment of Repentance fling
The Bird of Time has but a little way
To flutter—and the Bird is on the Wing

A Book of Verses underneath the Bough
A jug of Wine, a loaf of Bread—and Thou
Beside me singing in the Wilderness
Oh, Wilderness were Paradise enow

Some for the Glories of this World, and some
Sigh for the Prophet's Paradise to come
Ah, take the Cash, and let the Credit go
Nor heed the rumble of a distant drum

The worldly Hope men set their Hearts upon
Turns Ashes—or it prospers, and anon
Like Snow upon the Desert's dusty Face
Lighting a little hour or two—is gone

Look to the blowing Rose about us—'Lo
Laughing' she says, 'into the world I blow'
At once the silken tassel of my Purse
Tear, and its Treasure on the Garden throw

I sometimes think that never grows so red
The Rose as where some buried Caesar bled
That every Hyacinth the Garden wears
Dropt in her Lap from some once lovely Head

For some we loved, the loveliest and the best
That from his Vintage rolling Time hath prest
Have drunk their Cup a Round or two before
And one by one crept silently to rest

Alike for those who for Today prepare
And those that after some Tomorrow stare
A Muezzin from the Tower of Darkness cries
Fools! Your Reward is neither Here nor There

Why, all the Saints and Sages who discussed
Of the Two Worlds so wisely—they are thrust
Like foolish Prophets forth, their Words to Scorn
Are scattered, and their Mouths are stopt with Dust

Myself when young did eagerly frequent
Doctor and Saint, and heard great argument
About it and about, but evermore
Came out by the same door where I went

With them the seed of Wisdom did I sow
And with mine own hand wrought to make it grow
And this was all the Harvest that I reaped
I came like Water, and like Wind I go

Earth could not answer, nor the Seas that mourn
In flowing Purple, of their Lord forlorn
Nor rolling Heaven, with all his signs revealed
And hidden by the sleeve of Night and Morn

Then of Thee in Me works behind
The Veil, I lifted up my hands to find
A Lamp amid the Darkness, and I heard
As from Without—*Then Me Within Thee Blind*

Then to the lip of this poor earthen Urn
I leaned, the Secret of my Life to learn
And Lip to Lip it murmured—'While you live
Drink—for, once dead, you never shall return'

I think the Vessel, that with fugitive
Articulation answered, once did live
And drink, and Ah! The passive Lip I kissed
How may Kisses might it take—and give

For I remember stopping by the way
To watch a Potter thumbing his wet Clay
And with its all-obliterated Tongue
It murmured—'Gently, Brother, gently, pray'

And has not such a Story from of Old
Down Man's successive generations rolled
Of such a clod of saturated Earth
Cast by the Maker into Human mold

And not a drop that from our Cups we throw
For Earth to drink of, but may steal below
To quench the fire of Anguish in some Eye
There hidden—far beneath, and long ago

Waste not your Hour, nor in the vain pursuit
Of This and That endeavor and dispute
Better be jocund with the fruitful Grape
Than sadden after none, or bitter, Fruit

For 'Is' and 'Is-not' though with Rule and Line
And 'Up' and 'Down' by Logic I define
Of all that one should care to fathom
Was never deep in anything but—Wine

Ah, but my Computations, People say
Reduced the Year to better reckoning—Nay
'This was only striking from the Calendar
Unborn Tomorrow, and dead Yesterday'

And lately, by the Tavern Door agape
Came shining through the Dusk an Angel Shape
Bearing a Vessel on his Shoulder, and
He bid me taste of it, and it was—the Grape

Why, be this Juice the growth of God, who dare
Blaspheme the twisted tendril as a Snare
A Blessing, we should use it, should we not
And if a Curse—why, then, Who set it there

Strange, is it not, that of the myriads who
Before us passed the door of Darkness through
Not one returns to tell us of the Road
Which to discover we must travel too

Heaven but the Vision of fulfilled Desire
And Hell the Shadow from a Soul on fire
Cast on the Darkness into which Ourselves
So late emerged from, shall so soon expire

We are no other than a moving row
Of Magic Shadow—shapes that come and go
Round with the Sun-illumined Lantern held
In Midnight by the Master of the Show

But helpless Pieces of the Game He plays
Upon the Chequer-board of Nights and Days
Hither and thither moves, and checks and slays
And one by one back in the Closet lays

The Ball no question makes of Ayes and Noes
But Here or There as strikes the Player goes
And He that tossed you down into the Field
He knows about it all—He knows—He knows

The Moving Finger writes, and having writ
Moves on, nor all your piety or wit
Shall lure it back to cancel half a Line
Nor all your Tears wash out a Word of it

And that inverted Bowl they call the Sky
Where-under crawling cooped we live and die
Lift not your hands to It for help—for It
As impotently moves as you and I

With Earth's first Clay They did the Last Man knead
And there of the Last Harvest sowed the Seed
And the first Morning of Creation wrote
What the Last Dawn of Reckoning shall read

Yesterday This Day's Madness did prepare
Tomorrow's Silence, Triumph, or Despair
Drink, for you know not whence you came, nor why
Drink, for you know not why you go, nor where

And this I know, whether the one True Light
Kindle to Love, or Wrath consume me quite
One Flash of It within the Tavern caught
Better than in the Temple lost outright

Oh, Thou who Man of baser Earth didst make
And even with Paradise devise the Snake
For all the Sin wherewith the Face of Man
Is blackened—Man's forgiveness give—and take

And much as Wine has played the Infidel
And robbed me of my Robe of Honor—Well
I wonder often what the Vintners buy
One half so precious as the stuff they sell

Ye Ah, that Spring should vanish with the Rose
That Youth's sweet-scented manuscript should close
The Nightingale that in the branches sang
And, whence, and wither flown again, who knows

Would but some winged Angel ere too late
Arrest the yet unfolded Roll of Fate
And make the stern Recorder otherwise
En-register, or quite obliterate

And when like her, oh, Saki, you shall pass
Among the Guests Star-scattered on the Grass
And in your joyous errand reach the spot
Where I made One—turn down an empty Glass

Whose secret Presence, through Creation's veins
Running Quicksilver-like eludes your pains
Taking all shapes from Mah to Mahi, and
They change and perish all—but He remains

Whether at Nishapur of Babylon
Whether the Cup with sweet or bitter run
The Wine of Life keeps oozing drop by drop
The Leaves of Life keep falling one by one

Up from Earth's Centre through the seventh Gate
I rose, and on the Throne of Saturn sate
And many Knots unraveled by the Road
But not the knot of Human Death and Fate

Then to the rolling Heaven itself I cried
Asking, 'What Lamp had Destiny to guide
Her little children stumbling in the Dark'
And—'A blind understanding' Heaven replied

While the Rose blows along the River Brink
With old Khayyam the Ruby Vintage drink
And when the Angel with his darker Draught
Draws up to thee—take that, and do not shrink

The Vine has struck a Fibre, which about
It clings my Being—let the Sufi flout
Of my Base Metal may be filed a Key
That shall unlock the Door he howls without

Khayyam, who stitched the tents of science
Has fallen in grief's furnace and been suddenly burned
The Shears of Fate have cut the tent ropes of his life
And the broker of Hope has sold him for nothing

I myself upon a looser Creed
Have loosely strung the Jewel of Good deed
Let this one thing for my Atonement plead
That One for Two I never did misread

Shapes of all Sorts and Sizes, great and small
They stood along the floor and by the wall
And some loquacious Vessels were, and some
Listened perhaps, but never talked at all

Said one among them—'Surely not in vain
My substance of common Earth was taken
And to this Figure molded, to be broken
Or trampled back to shapeless Earth again'

Then said a Second—'Never a peevish Boy
Would break the Bowl from which he drank in joy
And He that with his hand the Vessel made
Will surely not in after wrath destroy'

After a momentary silence spake
Some Vessel of a more ungainly Make
'They sneer at me for leaning all awry
What, Did the Hand then of the Potter shake'

Whereat some one of the loquacious Lot
I think a Sufi pipkin-waxing hot
'All this of Pot and Potter—Tell me then
Who is the Potter, pray, and who the Pot'

'Why,' said another, 'Some there are who tell
Of one who threatens he will toss to Hell
The luckless Pots he marred in making—Pish
He's a Good Fellow, and it will all be well'

'Well!' Murmured one. 'Let whoso make or buy
My Clay with long Oblivion is gone dry
But fill me with the old familiar juice
Methinks I might recover by and by'

So while the Vessels one by one were speaking
The little Moon looked in that all were seeking
And then they jogged each other, 'Brother, Brother
Now for the Porter's shoulder-knot a-creaking'

Irem indeed is gone with all its Rose
And Jamshyd's Sev'n-ring'd Cup where no one knows
But still the Vine her ancient Ruby yields
And still a Garden by the water blows

Ah, with the Grape my fading Life provide
And wash my Body whence the life has died
And in a Winding-sheet of Vine-leaf wrapt
So bury me by some sweet Garden-side

CHAPTER FOUR

SA'ADI: Born in Shiraz 1207-1291

Last night my idol placed his hand upon my breast
He seized me hard and put a slave-ring in my ear
I said, 'Beloved', I am crying from your love
He pressed his lips on mine and silenced me
Anonymous Sufi Poem

A Sufi lives by the ethics of his own word and action, striving always to reach the abode of perfection. He has attained such nobility of character that he feels bountiful in poverty, content in hunger, cheerful in grief and friendly in hostility. He/she is possessed by this innate need to feed the hungry, to help the distressed, and to redress the wrongs of the aggrieved.

Sufis are of this world, and not of this world. Somewhat suspended like the clouds in mid-heaven. Sometimes, pouring showers of inspiration, and at times withholding the bolts of lightning in *understanding*, which might harm us due to our lack of perception. They are seized by this longing to enlighten the world, but can't pierce the veil of our limited intelligence, which has not experienced the delights of Mystical Path. And the Path is for the Seekers after Truth, whose behavior once they taste the wine of Truth, appears strange to us. *One of the Sufis by the name of Shibli, after experiencing the bliss of Union with his Beloved, was seen running through the streets carrying coals. He said he was going to set fire to Kabah, so that the Muslims would concern less about the place, and more about the Lord, Who is Everywhere!* This story is reminiscent of an old fable where truth stands out as a relative term, not something absolute and unchanging. A king complains that his subjects tell more lies than truth and wishes to establish a kingdom where everyone is trained to tell the truth. He devises a plan that every morning when the city gates are opened, everyone entering therein would be subject to a question, to which he has to reply truthfully.

In the public square gallows were erected for the ones to be hanged; who, if caught for not telling the truth, would suffer this stark humiliation. In the morning when the city gates were opened, the first one to walk in was a Sufi by the name of Nasrudin. The guard asked:

Where are you going? Tell me the truthfully, otherwise, you are sure to be hanged.

I am going to be hanged on those gallows. Nasrudin replied calmly.

I don't believe you. The guard scoffed.

Well, then, if I have told a lie, hang me! Nasrudin exclaimed mirthfully.

But then what you said would become the truth? Was the guard's flustered response!

Exactly! Your truth? Nasrudin sauntered away.

Another of Saadi's fables reveals the perception of *truth: I noticed an Arab sitting in the company of jewelers. He said, I had once lost my road in the desert and consumed all my food. I considered that I must perish when I suddenly caught sight of a bulging canvas bag. I shall never forget the joy and ecstasy I felt on thinking it might be parched grain, nor the despair and bitterness when I discovered it to be full of pearls.*

Saadi's full name was Sheikh Mushlihuddin, known as the Nightingale of Persia, who strove to right the wrongs of his own age and time, when religion was being torn into rags of bigotry and corruption, and false Sufis and dervishes were sprouting like the weeds. Not much is known about his life, but his two major works, Gulistan—the Rose Garden, and Bostan—the Kitchen Garden, are presumed to be autobiographical, lending us a few glimpses of his life through the curtain of Time. He compares the Heart to a flower that blooms in Beauty and spreads its Perfume. The first twenty years of his youth were spent at the Nizamiah College in Baghdad, where he studied, mastering Arabic in its purity of form and context. Then he traveled for thirty years from India in East to Syria in West. His first pilgrimage to Mecca was with his teacher Abdul-Kabir Gilani, and during his entire life he made about fourteen pilgrimages to Mecca. Finally, he returned to his hometown Shiraz, and devoted the latter part of his life to writing books and teaching his students. He had a great sense of humor, despite the fact that his life was rigged with hardships and tragedies.

At college, Saadi met a great Sufi master by the name of Surhawardi. After graduating, he had to flee Baghdad when the map of Iran and the whole of the Middle East were changing by the invasion of the Mongols, resulting in the fall of the Abbasid Empire. He went to central Asia and India, then to Yemen and Ethiopia through Mecca. Once, during his travels in Syria, he was captured by the Franks and sold as a slave to the Crusaders. Under their strict vigilance, he had to dig trenches in Tripoli until a Muslim merchant bought and freed him. But his previous slavery was replaced by another, since he had to marry the daughter of his benefactor. After his marriage, he went to North Africa and Anatolia before returning to Shiraz. He wrote profusely and feverishly till the end of his life, becoming the adored poet and mystic of Persia. Wit and wisdom kept him company even in his old age. One evening, in the market, he noticed a man who was looking to buy his book. Sa'adi asked the man what he liked about this author. The man who didn't know Sa'adi personally, said, *He is a funny man.* Sa'adi was pleased with this remark and gave his book for free to the man, who appreciated his humor.

Sa'adi died in Shiraz, and a tomb was built over his grave, which is now visited by many as some holy shrine. He is remembered as the Sufi of Shiraz and the Genius of Persia, whose love poetry and mystic parables still capture the hearts of millions.

Sufism is a voyage of discovery into ourselves! A pilgrimage to become the perfect servants of God. A love affair with the Divine Beloved in which the lovers merge in Mystical Union!

Love and ecstasy in Sufi poetry is the result of this Mystical Union with God, revealing the Link of Unity to All. A Unity which excludes not even one atom on this earth, where all created are the Creation of Love, and the sole purpose of this life is to journey on the Path of Love! Seeking the Face of Beloved in Everyone is a quest supreme, as if lifting the veils of Illusion and reaching the door of Awakening with joy in our hearts and light in our eyes to embrace Oneness. Sufi poems are the chariots of this Divine Quest, earthbound, yet reaching up to the heavens to gather more treasures of Love to share with the Loving Hearts.

Sufis are the friends of God. And a Sufi by the name of Khwaja Sahib in his thoughts on mysticism spills these pearls of wisdom in words:

A friend of God must have affection like the Sun. When the Sun rises, it is beneficial to all. All persons derive heat and light from it irrespective of whether they are Jews, Muslims, Christians, Buddhists, Hindus, Sikhs, etc.

A friend of God must be generous like an ocean or a river. We all get water from the sea or river to quench our thirst. No discrimination is made whether we are good or bad or whether we are a relation or a stranger.

A friend of God is one who has the quality of hospitality like the earth. We are raised and cradled in its lap, and it is always spread below our feet.

SAADI — BODY OF THE POET

Recline on the throne of heart
And with purity in manner be a Sufi

Deep in the sea are riches beyond compare
But if you seek safety, it is on the shore

Expect not faithfulness from nightingales
Who sing every moment to another rose

Like compasses we are, one foot stable in Islam
The other voyaging through all religions

I fear that you will not reach Mecca
O Nomad — For the road which you are
Following, leads to Turkestan

Worshiping God is not done with
Rosary beads, prayer carpet or robe
Worshiping God is serving people

If I were doing what I speak
I would be of a good conduct and devotee

Hast thou heard of how a Sufi drove
A few nails under his sandals
And an officer taking him by the sleeve
Said to him, 'Come and shoe my horse'

Nobody sees the thirsty pilgrims to Hijaz
Crowding at the bank of briny water
Wherever a sweet spring happens to be
Men, birds and insects flock around it

I behold whom I love, without an intervention
Then a trance befalls me, I lose the road
It kindles fire, then quenches it with a sprinkling shower

Wherefore thou seest me, burning and drowning
Whatever thou beholdest chants His praises
He knows this who has true perception
Not only the nightingale on the rosebush sings praises
But every bramble is a tongue, extolling Him

Turn not thy face from a sinner, o anchorite
Look upon him with benignity
If I am ignoble in my actions
Pass me by like a noble fellow

To the friends of God a dark night
Shines like the brilliant day
This felicity is not by strength of arm
Unless God the giver bestows it

The bird does not go to the grain displayed
When it beholds another fowl in the trap

Take advice by the misfortune of others
That others may not take advice from thee

When Loqman saw that in the hands of David
All iron became by miracle, soft like wax
He asked not, 'What art thou doing' because
He knew he would learn it without asking

Why should possessors of enjoyment and luck
Bear sorrow for fear of distress
Go, be merry, my heart-rejoicing friend
The pain of tomorrow must not be eaten today

As far as I am able I shall hold my heart
And if injured, I shall not injure in return
Though sugar may be thy food, as of a parrot
I shall sacrifice my sweet life to thy support

Wah, if the dead man were to return
Among his kinsfolk and connections
The refunding of the inheritance would be more painful
To the heirs than the death of their relative

Yesterday at dawn a bird lamented
Depriving me of sense, patience
Strength and consciousness
One of my intimate friends, who
Had perhaps heard my distressed voice
Said, 'I could not believe that thou
Wouldst be dazed by a bird's cry'
I replied, 'It is not becoming to humanity
That I should be silent when birds chant Praises'

The Friend is nearer to me than myself
But it is more strange that I am far from Him
What am I to do, to whom can it be said that He
Is in my arms, but I am exiled from him

I am that ant which is trodden underfoot
Not that wasp, the pain of whose sting causes lament
How should I give due thanks for the blessing
That I do not possess the strength of injuring mankind

Who appeared to thee like marrow, all pistachio
Was but skin upon skin like onion
Devotees with their face toward the world
Say their prayers with their back toward qiblah

Be thou well behaved, that a maligner
May not find occasion to speak of thy faults
When the harp is in proper tune
How can the hand of the musician correct it

O contentment, make me rich
For besides thee no other wealth exists
Loqman selected the corner of patience
Who has no patience, has no wisdom

Would that before my death
I could enjoy my wish
That a river's waves strike my knee
And I might fill my water-bag

My state is that of lightning
One moment it appears, and at another vanishes
I am sometime sitting in high heaven
Sometimes I cannot see the back of my foot
Were a Dervish always to remain in that state
He would not care for the Two Worlds
Of what use a dish of roses to thee
Take a leaf from my Rose Garden
A flower endures but five or six days
But this Rose Garden is always delightful

If someone asks me for His description
What shall I despairing say of one who has no form
The lovers have been slain by the beloved
No voice can come from the slain

The pretender sees no one but himself
Because he has the veil of conceit in front
If he were endowed with a God discerning eye
He would see that no one is weaker than himself

O bird of the morning, learn love from the moth
Because it burnt, lost its life, and found no voice
These pretenders are ignorantly in search for Him
Because he who obtained knowledge has not returned

O Thou who art above all imagination
Conjectures, opinions and ideas
Above anything people have said
Or we have read or heard
The assembly is finished
And life has reached its term
And we have, as at first
Remained powerless in describing Thee

A sweet-smelling piece of clay, one day in the bath
Came from the hand of a beloved one to my hand
I asked, 'art thou musk or ambergris'
Because thy delicious odor intoxicates me'
It replied, 'I was a despicable lump of clay
But for a while in the society of a rose
The perfection of my companion took affect on me
And if not, I am the same earth which I am'

I heard that a sheep had by a great man
Been rescued from the jaws and the power of a wolf
In the evening he stroked her throat with a knife
Whereon the soul of the sheep complained thus
'Thou hast snatched me away from the claws of a wolf
But at last I see thou art thyself a wolf'

Be not unconcerned, for, thou wilt be afflicted
If by thy hand a heart has been afflicted
Throw not a stone at the rampart of a fort
Because, possibly a stone may come from the fort

When thou seest a quarrel, be forbearing
Because gentlemen will shut the door of strife
Use kindness when thou seest contention
A sharp sword cannot cut soft silk
By a sweet tongue, grace and kindliness
Thou wilt be able to lead an elephant by a hair

Who lifts up his neck with pretensions
Foes hasten to him from every side
Sa'adi has fallen to be a hermit
No one came to attack a fallen man
First deliberation, then speech
The foundation was laid first, then the wall

The covering of the Kabah which is kissed
Has not been ennobled by the silkworm
It was some days in company with a venerable man
Wherefore it became respected like himself
Oh thou whose interior is denuded of piety
But wearest outwardly the garb of hypocrisy
Do not display a curtain of seven colors
Thou hast reed mats in thy house

When the calamity of time afflicts one limb
The other limbs cannot remain at rest
If thou hast no sympathy for the troubles of others
Thou art unworthy to be called by the name of man

I saw a mendicant at the door of Kabah
Who said this, and wept abundantly
'I ask not for the acceptance of my service

But for drawing the pen of pardon over my sins'

Of what use is thy frock, rosary and patched dress
Keep thyself free from despicable practices
Then thou wilt have no need for a cap of leaves
Have the qualities of a Dervish and wear a Tartar cap

Help the distressed in the day of prosperity
Because comforting the poor averts evil from thyself
When a mendicant implores thee for a thing
Give it, or else an oppressor may take it by force

If livelihood were increased by knowledge
None would be more needy than the ignorant
Nevertheless the ignorant receives a livelihood
At which the learned stand aghast
The luck of wealth consists not in skill
But only in the aid of heaven
It happens in the world that many
Silly men are honored and sages despised
If an alchemist has died in grief and misery
A fool discovered a treasure amidst ruins

Who opens to himself a door for begging
Will till he dies, remain a needy fellow
Abandon greediness and be a king
Because a neck without desire is high
I shall not let go my hold of Thy skirt
Even if Thou strike me with a sharp sword
After Thee I have no refuge, nor asylum
To Thee alone I shall flee, if I flee

Thou who art a slave to thy selfishness
Art mendacious in the game of love
If there be no way to reach the friend
Friendship demands to die in pursuit of it

I rise, as no other source is left to me
Though the foe may smite me with sword and arrow
If chance serves me I shall take hold of her sleeve
Or else I shall go and die on her threshold

The ill whishing eye, be it torn out
Sees only defects in his virtue
But if thou possesset one virtue and seventy faults
A friend sees nothing except that virtue

Would that those who are reproving me
Could see my face, o ravisher of hearts
That instead of a lemon in thy presence
They might heedlessly cut their hands

A virtuous and beauteous youth
Was pledged to a chaste maiden
I read that in the great sea
They fell into a vortex together
When a sailor came to take his hand
He said in anguish, from the waves
'Leave me' 'Take the hand of my love'
Whilst saying this, he despaired of life
In his agony he was heard to exclaim
Learn not the tale of love from the wretch
Who forgets his beloved in distress
Thus the lives of the lovers terminated
Learn from what has occurred that thou mayest know
Because Sa'adi is the way and means of love affairs
Well aware in the Arabian city of Baghdad
Tie your heart to the heart-charmer thou possessest
And shut thy eye to all the rest of the world
If Laila and Majnun were to come to life again
They might indite a tale of love on this occurrence

Listen to this story how in Baghdad
A flag and a curtain fell into dispute
Travel stained, dusty and fringed, the flag
Said to the curtain by way of reproach
'I and thou, we are both fellow servants
Slaves of the Sultan's palace
Not a moment had I rest from service
In season and out of season I traveled about
Thou hast suffered neither toil, nor siege
Not from the desert wind, nor dust and dirt
My step in the march is more advancing
Then why is thy honor exceeding mine
Thou art upon moon-faced servants
Or jasmine-scented girls
I have fallen into prentice hands
I travel with foot in fetters and head fluttering'
The curtain said, 'My head is on the Threshold'
Not like thine in the heavens
Who carelessly lifts up his neck
Throws himself upon his neck'

I spent my precious life in hopes, alas
That every desire of my heart will be fulfilled
My wishes were realized, but to what profit, since
There is no hope that my past life will return
The hand of fate has struck the drum of departure
O my two eyes, bid farewell to the head
O palm, forearm, and arm of my hand
All take leave from each other
For the last time, o friends, Pass near me
My life has elapsed in ignorance
I have done nothing, be on your guard

CHAPTER FIVE

A FEW PEARLS INSIDE THE OYSTER OF MYSTICISM

**RABIA
IBN AL ARABI
AL HALLAJ
FARID-UD-DIN
ATTAR**

*I will hide in my song
So that I may take kisses from your lips
As you sing it*
Abu Said

Whatever we wish to know well, we must love. We can't master any field of study — whether art, music, a profession, or an academic field — unless we love what we are studying. Study without love leads to a shallow, superficial understanding. Real mastery comes from love.

For many, Sufism is the path of love. To love others, to love the beauty of this world, develops the capacity to love. The more we can love, the more we can love God. To love God is to know God.

Many of us are afraid of love. We have been disappointed before, not only by our romantic loves, but also by friends and family we have loved. We can become afraid to open up and love again. There is an old Turkish saying: The one who was burnt by the soup blows on the yogurt. Yet whatever our past hurts and fears of future pain, we must learn to love again. One of the most important function of a teacher and a Sufi group of sincere seekers is to provide a safe place to risk loving.

Sufism is similar to Gnosticism, journeying in quest of divine knowledge and becoming one with God, Who is Everything. And yet it is different from Gnosis in a way that in Sufism knowledge is attained from within, not without. It is more of an Experience, sought by the seeker of a pure and loving heart, and attained by the Grace of God. In the words of Al Hallaj:

Gnosis is beyond the idea of beyond, and beyond spatial limit and beyond intention, and beyond awareness. And beyond received traditions, and beyond perception! Because all of these are something which was not in existence before being, and came into being in a place. God has never ceased to be, was and is before dimensions, causes and affect. So how can these dimensions contain Him, or limitations comprehend Him?

In other words, we have to step out of our limited self/intelligence, wipe clean the mirror of all impressions taught to us by creed, culture or religion, and draw within into the emptiness of our being, so that we could be receptive to the Light of Love, Truth, God.

Two stories in conformity with this *thought*. A man goes to a Sufi to be his disciple. He sits there and talks about all his studies and knowledge. The Sufi begins to pour tea into his cup and it is overflowing, which the man doesn't notice, since he is busy talking. Suddenly, he notices, reminding the Sufi that the cup is full. *Exactly, my point*. The Sufi responds. In order to learn our Way you need to empty your mind of all ideas and notions.

A man goes to a Sufi to be his disciple. The Sufi gives him a riddle to be solved by the end of the evening. The man returns with the answer. The Sufi tells him to come back after four years to be accepted as a disciple. The man is ecstatic, telling the gardener outside that he got lucky, because he was expecting at least ten years of wait, and only got four. Then he asked the gardener that if he didn't find the answer to the riddle, how many years would he had to wait?

You would have been accepted right away, if you didn't have the answer. The Gardener told him.

Some scholars believe that Sufis are the progeny of the Christian monks, the Catholic mystics and of the philosophers. Traditionally, the coffee which we drink was first used by the Sufis, to heighten awareness. In the words of Robert Graves: *We wear their clothes (shirt, belt, trousers), and we listen to their music (Andalusian, measured music, love songs; dance their dances (waltz, Morris dancing). Read their stories (Dante, Robinson Crusoe, Chaucer, William, etc.) We employ their esoteric phrases, (human spirit, moment of truth), and play their games, cards. We even belong to the derivations of their societies, Templars, Freemasonry, Masonic Orders.*

Rabia was the Mistress of the Masters, the early Sufis bowing before her wisdom with great reverence. She was born a century after the death of Prophet Muhammad. Her parents were poor. The night she was born, there was no oil to anoint the navel of the newborn daughter. Her mother begged her husband to borrow some oil from the neighbors, who went to them, but they didn't even open the door. The mother wept bitterly, and the father fell asleep in the corner. That night, he saw Prophet Muhammad in his dream, who told him that he shouldn't be sad, that this child would be the mediator for seventy thousand of his Community. The Prophet also instructed him to go to Isa Zadan, the governor of Basra, dictating this message to the Governor. *Every night you send upon me a hundred blessings and on Friday night four hundred! Last night was Friday night and you forgot me. To set right your forgetfulness, give this man four hundred dinars, which he has lawfully earned.* Upon awakening, the father constructed a letter from whatever he could remember from his dream, and took it to the governor of Basra. To his great astonishment, the governor gave him two hundred extra dinars, inviting him to come to him again if he needed more. The family lived in comfort until Rabia was about eleven year old, when her father died. The mother decided to journey to the outskirts of Basra to find work, but on the way bandits killed her, and Rabia along with her two older sisters was sold into slavery.

Rabia's master took her to Baghdad, trained her in singing and dancing, and made money out of her talents, while she sang and danced at the weddings. Years later when she was thirty-six and performing at a wedding celebration, she noticed that her songs were coming from her heart for her Beloved—true love for God had opened up her heart. From then on she refused to sing and dance for her master, who put a cord around her neck and took her to a slave market in Baghdad. One holy man purchased her freedom and gave her food and lodging. In the hermitage of this holy man Rabia prayed and fasted, and attained Union with her Beloved. After a few years, a Sufi by the name of Hasan al-Basri came to the hermitage and Sought Rabia's friendship. Soon, they became great friends and he proposed marriage. To which Rabia replied:

Marriage is for those who have being. But here being has disappeared, for I have become as nothing to my self, and I exist only through God, for I belong wholly to Him, and I live under the shadow of His control. You must ask for my hand from Him, not from me.

How did you find this Secret, Rabia? Hasan asked in awe, being himself a Seeker on the Path!

I lost all, found things in Him. Rabia replied

How did you come to know Him? Hasan asked in Sufic reverie.

You know of how, but I know of the how-less? Rabia replied, singing this quatrain.

> *I have made You the companion of my heart*
> *But my body is available to those who desire its company*
> *And my body is friendly toward its guest*
> *But the Beloved of my heart is the guest of my soul*

Rabia never married, but shared her wisdom and kindness who sought such treasures! During the discussions which she held frequently, the Sufi masters acknowledged her as the Queen of Sufism. When someone said, "We should surrender to the will of God," she would say, *what is there to surrender since everything belongs to Him.* If some Sufi talked about praying to God for opening the Door to Truth, she would add, *was the door ever closed?* Once Hasan talked about the long Journey of Life toward the gates of Death! She sent him, the next day, a hair, a needle and a piece of wax, with a note attached. *Be like wax and illumine the world, and burn yourself. Be like a needle and work naked. When you have done these two things for a thousand years you will be like a hair.*

Hasan, once saw Rabia near the lake. Throwing his prayer rug on top of the water, he said. *Come, Rabia, let's pray here, together.*

When you are showing off your spiritual goods in the worldly market, it should be things which your fellow men cannot display. Rabia tossed her prayer rug into the air, herself perched on it. Then alighted, seeing the sadness in Hasan's eyes. *Hasan, let's not boast of our spiritual powers. What you did fishes can do, and what I did flies can do.*

Every day, Rabia went to Al Aqsa mosque to pray and teach whoever came to seek her love and wisdom. She could never tire of talking about love. *Love has come from eternity and passes into eternity, and none has been found in seventy thousand worlds who drinks one drop of it, until at last he is absorbed in God.*

After her death, her followers built a tomb for her, which still exists near the Christian Church of the Ascension on top of the Mountain of Olives.

RABIA—Born in the city of Basra in Iraq
717-802

O God, if I worship You
For fear of Hell, burn me in Hell
If I worship You in hope of Paradise
Exclude me from Paradise
But if I worship You for Your Own sake
Grudge me not Your everlasting Beauty

I love You with two loves—a selfish love
And a Love that You are worthy of
As for the selfish love, it is that I think of You
To the exclusion of everything else
And as for the Love that You are worthy of
Ah! That I no longer see any creature
But I see only You
There is no praise for me in either of these loves
But the praise in both is for You

Everyone prays to You from fear of the Fire
And if You do not put them in the Fire
This is their reward
Or they pray to You for the Garden
Full of fruits and flowers
And that is their prize
But I do not pray to You like this
For I am not afraid of the Fire
And I do not ask you for the Garden
But all I want is the essence of Your Love
And to return to be One with You
And to become Your Face

O God, my whole occupation
And all my desire in this world
Of all worldly things
Is to remember You
And in the Hereafter
It is to meet You
This is on my side, as I have stated
Now You do whatever You will

In love, nothing exists between breast and Breast
Speech is born out of longing
True description from the real taste
The one who tastes, knows
The one who explains, lies
How can you describe
The true form of Something
In whose presence you are blotted out
And in whose being you still exist
And who lives as a sign of your journey

Your hope in my heart is the rarest treasure
Your Name on my tongue is the sweetest word
My choicest hours
Are the hours I spend with You
Oh, God, I can't live in this world
Without seeing Your face
I am a stranger in Your country
And lonely among Your worshippers
This is the substance of my complaint

Your prayers are your light
Your devotion is your strength
Sleep is the enemy of both
Your life is the only opportunity
That life can give you
If you ignore it, if you waste it

You will only turn to dust
Chained by love
Captured again
Struggle is futile
Escape is impossible

Love is a sea
With unseen shores
With no shores at all
The wary don't dive in
To swim in love
Is to drink poison
And find it sweet
I struggled like a wild mare
Drawing the noose tighter

O God, whatsoever You have apportioned
To me of worldly things
Give that to Your enemies
And what You have apportioned
To me in the Hereafter
Give that to Your Friends
For You suffice me

I won't serve God
Like a laborer expecting wages

Ibn-Al Arabi is the intellectual universe of Sufi Creed and Thought. He was only eight when his family moved from Spain to Seville. At the age of fifteen, he experienced an extraordinary power of revelation, which he explained later in his works as unveiling of Truth. This was the time he met with Averroes (Avecina)—a commentator of Aristotle and an Arab philosopher of Spain. Then he went to Mecca, and on his way to Anatolia met several sages and Sufis. He settled in Damascus, where he wrote extensively. There, he made friendship with another Sufi, Makin-al Din, whose sister also influenced him in Sufic pursuits, and he named her,

Mistress of Hijaz. But, it was Makn-al Din's daughter, Nezam, who inspired him to write his famous collection of Sufi poems. Ibn-Al Arabi, even in his youth, claimed the bliss of Union with his Beloved. He says, *the Perfect Knowledge of God involves seeing with both eyes; the eye of reason, and the eye of unveiling,* which he calls imagination. *Divine Wisdom,* he says, *is associated with a different divine attribute. Hence, each prophet represents a different mode of knowing and experiencing the reality of God.* He was a prolific writer, leaving about three thousand pages of wisdom for his students after his death, and was buried in Damascus.

IBN AL-ARABI
Born in the town of Murcia in Spain
1165-1240

My heart has opened unto every form
It is a pasture for gazelles
A cloister for Christian monks
A temple for idols
The Kaaba of the pilgrim
The tablets of the Torah
And the Book of the Quran
I practice the religion of Love

Someone asked me, 'What is lover-hood'
I replied, 'Don't ask me about these things
When you become like me, you will know
When it calls you, you will tell its tale
What it is to be a lover, to have perfect thirst
So let me explain the water of life'

They journeyed
When the darkness of night
Had let down her curtain
And I said to her
'Pity a passionate lover
Outcast and distraught

When desires eagerly encompass
And at whom
Speeding arrows are aimed
Wheresoever he bends his course'
She displayed her teeth
And lightning flashed
And I knew not
Which of the twain rent the gloom
And I said
'Is it not enough for him
That I am in his heart
And that he beholds me
At every moment
Is it not enough'

If I bow to her as is my duty
And if she never returns my salutation
Have I just cause for complaint
Lovely woman feels no obligation

God made the creatures
As veils, he who knows them to be such
Is led back to Him
But he who takes them as real
Is barred from
His Presence
God is your mirror
In which you contemplate yourself
And you are His mirror
In which He contemplates
His Divine Attributes

Al Hallaj is the first martyr of Sufism, being executed most brutally for proclaiming, *I am the Truth. I am God*. At an early age he studied Arabic and Quran. He got married, had one son. He associated with many mystics of his time, but broke away from them. He went to Mecca for a pilgrimage, and returned to settle in Basra. He is accused of playing the Jesus, as if immolating his life, not only for the sins of the Muslims, but for the whole human race. One day, in a mystical trance, he exclaimed on the street, *I am the Truth.*

For this heresy, as it was viewed in that time and age, he was arrested and executed. His executioner, later, described his dream, in which he saw Al Hallaj in Paradise. The executioner asks God, *why is Pharaoh in hell, for saying, I am God, while Al Hallaj saying the same thing is in Paradise.* God says, *When Pharaoh spoke those words, he thought only of himself and forgot Me. But when Al Hallaj said those words, he had forgotten himself and thought only of Me.* Now, he is venerated, demonstrating through his works that Love means suffering for the sake of others.

AL HALLAJ
Born in Baghdad between 858-922

Love is to stand before your Beloved
Stripped naked of all attributes
So that his qualities become your
Qualities
Between you and me there lingers
'it is I'
Which torments me
Ah, lift through mercy this
'it is I'
From between us both

I am he whom I desire, whom I desire is I
We are two spirits dwelling in a single body
If you see me, you have seen me
And if you see him, you have seen us
Now stands no more
Between the Truth and me
Or seasoned demonstration
Or proof of revelation
Now, brightly blazing full

Truth's luminary
That drives out sight
Each flickering, lesser light

My Beloved takes no blame
He gave me wine and lavished
Much attention upon me
Like a host caring for a guest
After some time had passed
He called for a sword
And the execution mat
This is the reward for those
Who drink old wine
With an old lion
In the heat of summer

Kill me, o my trusty friends
For in my killing is my life
My life is in my death
And my death is in my life

Attar means perfume. Farid-ud-din adopted this name as his pen name in conformity with his profession, because he was a perfume maker. Attar was a wealthy man, his perfume business flourishing. One day a dervish walked into his shop, staring at everything in amazement. Attar asked him why he was staring at his wares in some sort of shock and disbelief. The dervish answered:

I am wondering how you are going to die when you have to leave all this wealth behind?

I will die just as you will, Attar responded impatiently.

But I have nothing to worry about. All I have is the cloak on my back and this begging bowl. Now, do you still claim that you will die the way I will? The dervish looked into his eyes piercingly.

Of course. Attar was fascinated, his heart fluttering all of a sudden.

Upon hearing this, the dervish uttered the name of God. Using his begging bowl as a pillow he lay down and died. Now, Attar was the one in shock, his heart caught in flames of pain and love he had not ever known before. Soon after he closed his business and joined the circle of the Sufis. After a few years he went on a pilgrimage to Mecca. He returned to Persia consumed by the fire of Mystical Inspiration, writing poetry and stories.

His Sufi ideal is that the goal of the Quest is for Self to step aside, and to let the Absolute know Itself through Itself. From multiplicity-in-unity to unity-in-multiplicity, one must die before dying. Not a biological death, but a spiritual one, where the soul dies, and by dying is transformed, and then returns to the material world. The sensory and psychic forces disappear and the vision of unity fills the emptied soul. This is when one sees God in Oneness. Then one returns to the consciousness of multiplicity, the spirit returns to all things.

Attar's most famous work is the allegorical poem, *The Conference of the Birds*. A group of birds, representing various human types traverse seven immense valleys on their journey to the Simurgh—the mythical bird, which represents the Supreme Being. The valleys are named by Attar as those of the Quest, Love, Understanding, Detachment, Unity, Bewilderment and Extinction. On finding and contemplating the majestic and beautiful Simurgh, the birds achieve their essential and eternal life and identity by annihilating their individual selves in Him. And they find themselves in Him as if One and the Same, a reflection of Reality into the Real.

Some Israelites insulted Jesus one day as he walked through the marketplace. He answered them only by repeating prayers in their name. Someone said to him "You prayed for these men. Do you not feel anger at their vile treatment of you?" Jesus answered, *I could spend only what I carry in my purse.* Attar stressed the point of love with this anecdote in one of his stories.

Attar died a tragic death. He was captured by the hands of one of the Genghis Khan's soldiers during the Mongol invasion of Persia. The story goes, as he was being dragged away, someone came along and offered the Mongol a thousand pieces of silver for Attar. Attar advised the Mongol not to accept because the price was not right. The Mongol, heeding the words of Attar, refused to sell him. A while later, another man came by, offering a sack of straw for Attar. Attar told the Mongol to sell him now, for that was the worth of his life. The Mongol was enraged and cut off Attar's head. So died the great Sufi, teaching another lesson in selflessness to the seekers of Truth, even in his death!

ATTAR—Born in Nishapur in Persia
1136-1230

Come you lost atoms, to your Center draw
And be the eternal Mirror that you saw
Rays that have wandered into Darkness wide
Return and back into your Sun subside

The sea was asked
Why it was dressed in blue
The color of mourning
And why it became agitated
As if fire made it boil
It answered
The blue robe spoke of the sadness
Of separation from the Beloved
And it was the fire of love
Which made it boil
Yellow is the color of gold
The alchemy of the Perfected Man
The sea added
Who is refined, until
He is in a sense Gold

The sun of my Perfection is a Glass
Wherein from Seeing into Being pass
All who, reflecting as reflected see
Themselves in Me, and Me in them, not Me
But all of Me, that a contracted Eye
Is comprehensive of Infinity
Not yet Themselves; no Selves, but of All
Fractions, from which they split and whither fall

As water lifted from the Deep, again
Falls back in individual Drops of Rain
Then melts into the Universal Main
All you have been, and seen, and done, and thought
Not You but I, have seen and been and wrought
I was the Sin that from Myself rebelled
I the Remorse that toward Myself compelled
Sin and contrition—Retribution owed
And cancelled—Pilgrim, Pilgrimage, and Road
Was but Myself toward Myself, and your
Arrival but Myself at my own Door
Rays that have wandered into Darkness wide
Return, and back into your Sun subside

His beauty if it thrill thy heart
If thou a man of passion art
Of time and eternity
Of being and non-entity
Ask not
When thou hast passed the bases four
Behold the sanctuary door
And having satisfied thine eyes
What in the sanctuary lies
Ask not
The Heavenly Tablet and the Pen
Are certainly thy tongue and brain
Do thou the pen and tablet know
But of the Pen and Tablet, O
Ask not
Thy breast in the Celestial Throne
And Heaven the heart that it doth own
Yet but a cipher are the twain
And what the cipher is, again
Ask not
When unto this sublime degree
Thou hast attained, desist to be

But lost to self in nothingness
And, being not, of more and less
Ask not
Be thou a particle of shade
Whereon the sun's light is displayed
And when thou shalt no longer be
Of happiness and misery
Ask not
Attar, if thou hast truly come
Unto this place, that is thy home
In thy enjoyment of the Truth
Do thou of anguish and of ruth
Ask not

The Sun can only be seen
By the light of the Sun
The more
A man or woman knows
The greater
The bewilderment
The closer to the Sun
The more dazzled
Until a point is reached
Where one no longer is

A mystic knows without knowledge
Without intuition or information
Without contemplation
Or description or revelation
Mystics are not themselves
They do not exist in selves
They move as they are moved
Talk as words come
See with sight
That enters their eyes

I met a woman once
And asked
Where love had led her
Fool, there is no destination
To arrive at
She cried
Loved one and lover
And Love
Are infinite

Your face is neither infinite nor ephemeral
You can never see your own face
Only a reflection, not the face itself
So you sigh in front of mirrors
And cloud the surface
It's better to keep your breath cold
Hold it, like a diver does in the ocean
One slight movement, the mirror-image goes
Don't be dead or asleep or awake
Don't be anything
What you most want
What you travel around wishing to find
Lose yourself as lovers lose themselves
And you will be That

The whole world is a marketplace for Love
For naught that is, from Love remains remote
The Eternal Wisdom made all things in Love
On Love they all depend, to Love all turn
The earth, the heavens, the sun, the moon and the stars
The center of their orbit find in Love
By Love are all bewildered, stupefied
Intoxicated by the Wine of Love
From each, Love demands a mystic silence
What do all seek so earnestly, 'tis Love
Love is the subject of their inmost thoughts

In Love no longer 'Thou' and 'I' exist
For self has passed away in Beloved
Now will I draw aside the veil from Love
And in the temple of my inmost soul
Behold the Friend, Incomparable Love
He who would know the secret of both worlds
Would find the secret of them both in Love

CHAPTER SIX

SUFI MYSTICS AND PROPHETS

SARMAD—Born in Kashan in Iran, west of Turkey and Iraq and Afghanistan and Pakistan. 1590-1660
   ST. JOHN OF THE CROSS—Born in Castile in Spain. 1542-1591
   PROPHET MUHAMMAD—Born in Mecca in Hijaz. 570-632

God, Thou dwelleth in Kaaba and Somnath
And in the enamored lover's heart
Thou art the rose and also the amorous nightingale
Thou art the moth on Thine own beauty's taper
Prince Dara Shikoh

Sufis of the world are countless, but these three chosen in this chapter belong to the Order of the major world religions, Judaism, Christianity and Islam. Collectively, they are known as the People of the Book. They not only claim the Creed of Love, but proclaim the Bliss of Union with the Beloved. Their Journey in Life has been their quest for the Divine. Many Sufis and saints have claimed to have seen the Lord or the Beloved, but only Prophet Muhammad and St. John of the Cross (historically and metaphorically) have made the claim to Mystical Night Journey, as the unveiling of Mysticism in Word and Thought. Sarmad's Mystical Journey, on the other hand, is Visible and Timeless, both earthly and heavenly. He clings to his earthly beloved like a shadow, yet his soul soars high to kiss the lips of the Divine Beloved.

Amongst the Sufis have been former Zoroastrian. Many Jews, Arabs, Hindus, Christians, Egyptians, Spaniards and Englishmen are the claimants of Sufi ideal and practice. *A Sufi literalist Would be able to swallow a hundred oceans, worship idols while not worshipping them, travel to China in a state of drunkenness—being in the world and yet not of it—not to mention his hundred suns and moons,* as Idries Shah explains it.

To quote Margaret Smith, the first Sufi lodge was built in Ramla in Syria.

One day a Christian prince had gone hunting. While on the road he saw two Sufis meet and embrace each other. They then sat down at the same spot, spreading out what food they had, and eating together. Their affection for each other pleased the prince, and he called out to one of them and asked him who the other was. The man replied, *I don't know.*

The prince said, *What relation is he to you?*

The man answered, *None at all.*

The prince asked *From what place has he come?*

He said, *I don't know that either.*

The prince said, *Why then do you show each other such affection?*

The dervish replied, *He belongs to my Way.*

The prince asked, *Have you any place where you can meet together?* When the dervish said they had not, the prince said, *I will build you such a place.* And so he did.

Sufi Ideal by Bistami:

Try to gain one moment in which you see only God on earth and in heaven. Be in a realm where neither good, nor evil exists.

Both of them belong to the world of Created beings; in the presence of Unity there is neither command, nor prohibition.

A single atom of sweetness of wisdom in man's heart is better than a thousand pavilions in Paradise.

What is the way to God? Leave the Way, and you have arrived at God.

I went from God to God, until they cried from me in me, 'O Thou, I.'

A Sufi delves into the pool of his/her own inner duality, where men and women are the same. The meaning of the form does not differ, for the principles soul/spirit, masculine/feminine exist in both, irrespective of the outer form. The first stage to Awakening is the existence of the passionate soul, the soul which demands *understanding*. The second stage is the feminine principle, the spirit accusing the Self of its imperfections, where the war is waged between good and evil. The third stage is the masculine principle, the soul longing to end the battle of evil and good. Peace is declared only when the spirit/feminine is united with the soul/masculine, as if consumed in the Fire of Love, and resurrected in the Eternal Flame of Unity and Bliss.

Know that the Absolute cannot be contemplated independently of a concrete being, and it is more perfectly seen in human form than in any other, and more perfectly in woman than in man. Ibn Al-Arabi

Sarmad means eternal or everlasting, he was born of rich Jewish parents. He studied Judaic Scriptures, but his longing to know truth led him to study other religions, especially, Islam. After reading the Quran, he became a Muslim, adopting the name of Mohammad Sayed. Still restless and searching, he decided to travel and learn more about other faiths. His parents agreed to send him to distant lands as a merchant, where he could trade carpets, textile goods and ceramic vases for gold and silver. As a rich merchant, he landed into India with the prospect of accruing more riches, but fate took a strange turn and he scattered his riches to the winds. One day in the bazaar he saw a Hindu boy by the name of Abhu Chand, and fell so madly in love with him that his heart was torn open with the Light of Divine Love. Abhu Chand became his Medium to find his True Beloved Who had eluded him so far. Abandoning his wealth, even his clothes, he wandered on the streets naked, singing verses divine, and not resting until the parents of Abhu Chand allowed their son to be with him; understanding, that his love for their son was spiritual, not physical. From then on, he became known as Naked Sarmad, accompanied by his Beloved, Abhu Chand in all the splendor of jewels and fineries, a strange pair they were. He was being revered as a saint, doling out a wealth of poetry, and even performing miracles. He attracted the attention of Prince Dara Shikoh, who was the son of the emperor Shah Jahan—the architect of Taj Mahal. Dara Shikoh himself was a Sufi and a mystic, discovering a true Sufi in the poetry of Naked Sarmad. Shah Jahan himself was not impressed, and sent his vizier to find about Sarmad before he could allow his princely son to befriend this Sufi/sage. The vizier returned with the couplet of his own:

Sarmad's famous miracles work by fits and starts
The only revelation is of his private parts.

The rest is history—to be explained while we read his verses, since Sarmad is one of my favorite Sufis, included in my book, Glorious Taj and Beloved Immortal.

SARMAD

We have forgotten all the books we read
Only the text of love rings in our head

I am all things, a child of heaven and hell
Monk, priest and rabbi, Muslim and infidel

O Sarmad, it is the Lord's nature
To shower compassion and grace
Look at the crack of lightning
And the downpour of rain
And see how little is His ire
And how abounding His Grace

O Sarmad, in this world you bore the palm
From infidelity you turned toward Islam
But after all what short-comings
Did you notice in Allah and Prophet
That you turned away from them
And became a devotee of Lakshaman and Ram

Convinced of the Truth of His mysteries who became
More expansive than the firmament he became
Mullahs say, 'Ahmed went to heaven'
But says Sarmad that into Ahmed heaven came

He who gave thee the world of sovereignty
Gave me all the accessories of anxiety and poverty
He clad in garments those with evils
Upon the impeccable He bestowed the robe of nudity

In youth Satan's strength could not touch me
From the dust of my sins my garment remained free
At the approach of senility, however, sins acquired youthful vigor
Resulting in a peculiar anguish, but came forth no remedy

A stumbling block is your planning ray
The wilds of worries are with a leopard's danger fraught
Know destiny as strong and endeavor as weak
This strength and this weakness be at war let not

I know not if in this spherical old monastery
My God is Abhu Chand or someone else

O Sarmad, he who attained divine Love
And lost body-consciousness through the Wine of Love
Could not be made conscious even by the executioner's sword
Nay, he attained the rank of Muhammad above

Having lost my existence, I know not what it is
I have become a spark, which knows not what smoke is
I have sacrificed my all, my heart, my life, my faith
The bargain is struck, but I know not what the gain is

None other than good are sacrificed at the Lover's altar
Mind of poor qualities and evil-minded find no place at that altar
Yourself being a true lover, be not afraid of death
The dead-hearted are never led to that altar

Like the word and its meaning, regard Him and me
Like the eye and the eyesight separate and yet united
Regard Him and me
Not for a moment do we ever become separate
From one another
Like the flower and its fragrance everywhere
Regard Him and me

I recognize Thee my Friend
Thou hast come
In the form of a naked sword
To embrace me

We opened our eyes from eternal sleep, awakened by the din
But it was still an evil night, and so we slept again

*St. John of the Cross is the most sublime of all Spanish Sufis/mystics, who
sings of Divine Love from the lips of God Himself, it seems.* He learned the
importance of love from his parents. His father gave up status and
wealth when he married a weaver's daughter, and was disowned by his
family. After his father died, he and his mother suffered great poverty, at
times, suffering the pangs of hunger in the wealthiest city of Spain. John
started working when he was fourteen in order to support himself and
his mother. Then he joined the Carmelite Order at the request of Saint
Teresa of Avila to preach the life of Prayer and Spirituality. But many of
the men of his own Carmelite Order felt threatened by the nobility of his
spirit, and kidnapped him. He was locked in a cell six feet by ten feet and
beaten three times a week by the monks. There was only one tiny
window high up near the ceiling. Yet in that unbearable cell of cold and
desolation, his love and faith were like fire and light. He had nothing left
but God, and God brought him his greatest of joys in the seclusion of
darkness. After nine months, John made his escape by unscrewing the
lock on his door, and creeping past the guards, unnoticed. During this
time of torture and suffering, he had written great poems of mystical
beauty, which he carried with him, on the road to freedom. He had no
idea where he was, only following a dog toward the rungs of liberty and
struggle. He hid himself in a convent infirmary, where he read his poems
to the nuns. Love had been the quest of his life, always searching for the
Beloved, and he had found Him in the prison of hopeless, helpless Pain.
He had prayed and suffered, longing for the union with God, and when
that Gift was granted to him by the Grace of God, he had let his ecstasy
express itself in the words, Dark Night of the Soul. To read this poem is
to feel his joy; perhaps, tasting the bliss, which might reveal to us the
Beautiful Door of Love in all its manifestations.

House in the poem is Soul, *Darkness* the Spirit, *Secret ladder* the
Longing, etc.

ST. JOHN OF THE CROSS

On a dark night, Kindled in love with yearnings
Oh, happy chance
I went forth without being observed
My house being now at rest
In darkness and secure, by the secret ladder, disguised
Oh, happy chance
In darkness and in concealment
My house being now at rest
In the happy night, in secret, when none saw me
Nor I beheld aught, without light or guide
Save that which burned in my heart
This light guided me, more surely than the light of noonday
To the place where He (well I knew Who)
Was awaiting me
A place where none appeared
Oh, night that guided me
Oh, night more lovely than the dawn
Oh, night that joined Beloved with lover
Lover transformed in the Beloved
Upon my flowery breast
Kept wholly for himself alone
There He stayed sleeping, and I caressed Him
And the fanning of the cedars made a breeze
The breeze blew from the turret as I parted His locks
His gentle hand wounded around my neck
And caused all my senses to be suspended
I remained lost in oblivion
My face I reclined on the Beloved
All ceased and I abandoned myself
Leaving my cares forgotten
Among the lilies

The Creed of the Sufis itself proclaims Prophet Muhammad as the first Sufi of Islam, not that he claimed to be one, but by studying his life through Hadith and Quran. A few quotes of his sayings from the Hadith confirm the claim of the Sufis.

He who hears the voice of the Sufi people and does not say Amen, is recorded in God's presence as one of the heedless.

God said: I who cannot fit into universes upon universes, fit into the heart of the sincere believer. The heart is a temple that can house God. All hearts are temples, and to open our hearts is to allow in the divine presence.

I would like to be a bridge over the fire (hell) so that creatures might pass over me and not be harmed by it.

Most of the people of Paradise are fools, but Highest Heaven is for those who possess Inner Heart.

By pious fools my back hath been broken.

Sufis also claim to have learned the dance of the *Whirling Dervishes* from Prophet Muhammad by recounting this story. A poet by the name of Ka'ab went to the mosque in Medina to listen to Prophet Muhammad's sermon. After listening to the Prophet's words, he fell into ecstasy, and started reciting a poem about his newfound love for God and God's Messenger. The Prophet, in turn, began to dance. His right hand was turned palm up toward heaven, and his left hand was turned palm down to earth. *This symbolizes receiving inspiration and divine blessings with the right hand and the teaching and spreading of these blessings with the left hand. This is the same hand position that the Mevlevi Dervishes use today. Then dervishes take what they receive from God and give it to others.*

Quran is another source for the Sufis to magnify the belief/knowledge of The Night of Power, or, *Night Journey*, which transported the Prophet in an instant from Mecca to Jerusalem through all heavens to the Presence of the Beloved, before he returned to the earth. A verse concerning this Night Journey was revealed to the Prophet Muhammad after he had returned from the dazzling light of Union and Bliss. This Night Journey, as related by the Sufis and historians, is sublime and beautiful, though the verse itself is simple.

The Night Journey
Glory be to Him
Who carried His servant by Night
From the sacred temple of Mecca

To the Temple that is Remote
Whose precinct We have blessed
That We might show him of Our signs
For He is the Hearer and the Seer. Quran 17:1

Sufi poetry also claims its origin from the poetical splendor of the Quran, though Prophet Muhammad is not the author, only the Vessel, heeding the Voice of the Beloved. The one verse cited in this chapter is the most beloved of the Sufi Poets, who are guided by this on the Mystical Path to meet the Beloved. Prince Dara Shikoh, the Sufi, interprets it most beautifully:

Niche applies to the world of bodily existence, the *Lamp* to the Light of Essence and *Glass* to the human Soul, which is like a shining star and that, on account of this lamp, the Glass also appears like a Lamp. That Lamp is lit, applies to the Light of Essence, while the *Blessed Tree* refers to the Self of the Truth. Holy and Exalted is He, who is free from the limitations of the east and west. By olive oil is meant the Great Soul, which is neither of eternity past, nor of eternity to come; in that the *Olive* is a sacred tree, luminescent and resplendent by itself, and possessing great purity and elegance, and requiring no medium of fire to be lighted! Glass of the Soul is so luminous that it need not be touched with the fire of human world, possessing inherent fire of its own to Seek Love and Beloved. *Light upon Light* signifies that Purity of His Light is so dazzling that no one can behold it with a naked eye, unless He Himself guides with the Light of His Unity. To be precise, God is manifest with the Light of His Essence in elegant and refulgent curtains and there is no veil or darkness concealing Him.

After the Quranic revelation about the Night Journey, one of the bitterest opponents of Prophet Muhammad by the name of Abu Jahl teased him that how could he make the journey to heaven when he can't even lift his two feet up without falling to earth. The Prophet's response, *I didn't say I went, I said I was taken.*

Prince Dara Shikoh views this Night Journey of the Prophet as a mystical leap into the quantum world, where ether is the only Medium for the soul to travel with the speed of lightning.

Since soul is subtler than air, there is no wonder that the famous journey to the heaven made by the Prophet was in his physical body. And nothing to wonder, if Jesus still lives in the heaven in his physical body! For our souls are bodies, and our bodies are souls. Dara Shikoh.

PROPHET MUHAMMAD

Allah is the Light
Of the heavens and the earth
The similitude of His Light
Is as a lustrous Niche Wherein is the Lamp
The Lamp is in a Glass
The Glass as if it were a Glittering Star
This Lamp is lit by a Blessed Tree
An Olive
Neither of the east, nor of the west
Whose oil will well-nigh glow forth
Though fire toucheth it not
Light upon Light
Allah guides to His Light
Whomsoever He wills
Allah sets parables for men
Allah knows all things full well
The Quran — Al Nur 24:36

CHAPTER SEVEN

The Prophet of Lebanon
Khalil Gibran
Born in Bsharri, Lebanon
1883-1931

Drink to me only with thine eyes
And I will pledge with mine
Or leave a kiss but in the cup
And I'll not look for wine
The thirst that from the soul doth rise
Doth ask a drink divine
But might I of Jove's nectar sup
I would not change for thine
I sent thee late a rosy wreath
Not so much honoring thee
As giving it a hope, that there
It could not withered be
But thou thereon didst only breathe
And sent'st it back to me
Since when it grows, and smelts, I swear
Not of itself, but thee   Ben Jonson

Seek ye first the Kingdom of Heaven, and all these things will be added unto you.

This Kingdom of Heaven in Bible is the holy abode of all Seekers in all walks of life, who aspire to walk on the Road of Love to be united with the Beloved. Sufis, saints, mystics and philosophers have walked on this Road, choosing different Paths, but reaching the same destination, which is the Throne of God.

Allah hath treasures beneath the Throne, the keys whereof are the tongues of the poets.

These treasures mentioned in Hadith, though not sought by the Seekers, are bestowed upon them when they enter the Kingdom of

Heaven. They become the vessels of Divine Inspiration, offering us the scent of Love, and guiding us on the Path to Unity.

Sufis are Mystics and Mystics are Sufis as the pilgrims on this Road, since they are the lovers of God and Mankind. Yet Mankind's love for defining and setting boundaries has drawn a thin line to settle them in their separate abodes of Light and Enlightenment.

Sufi is the one who begins his/her journey to the Kingdom of Heaven through the Fire of Love in his/her inner Heart.

Mystic is the one who begins his/her journey to the Kingdom of Heaven through the Fire of Love in his/her inner Eye of the psyche.

When the inner Eye or Heart of the Seekers attains the knowledge of Infinite Consciousness, they strive to share the pearls of their wisdom with the whole world. Those precious gems in prose or poetry are scattered before us indiscriminately, the priceless bounties of Divine Inspiration, for us to cherish and to nurture love, kindness compassion, dissolving all boundaries of race, creed, color or religion. The first step toward this goal is to journey far and wide to meet a few Sufis and Mystics. *Happy wanderings into the land of the Sufis and the Mystics!*

Khalil Gibran was born in a small town of Bsharri in the cedar grove of North Lebanon. His mother was the daughter of a Maronite priest, so he was baptized by his grandfather, employing the rites of Roman Catholic Church from Antioch. He had one half-brother, Peter, by his mother's first marriage. She had married young and had moved to Brazil, where Peter was born, but then her husband had died and she had returned to Lebanon. From her second marriage, Khalil Gibran was born, six year younger than Peter, preceded by two sisters, Mariana and Sultana, two and four years younger than him, respectively.

Khalil Gibran was greatly influenced by his mother who was well-read and well-educated, being proficient in both French and Arabic. At eleven years of age, Khalil Gibran had memorized all the psalms, his love for books and nature cultivated by his mother. Since Lebanon was under Turkish rule, and many families fleeing under the brunt of taxes and tyranny, Khalil Gibran's family had decided to find fortunes on the gold-paved streets of America. Khalil Gibran was only twelve year old when his family moved to New York, with the exception of his father who didn't want to leave Lebanon. Peter was eighteen year old, so he secured a job in a grocery store in Boston to support the family. Khalil Gibran went to school in Boston for two years, then returned to Lebanon to complete his studies.

Besides studying, Khalil Gibran loved to study nature, befriending the holy cedars of Lebanon, and always longing for solitude and contemplation. He had just turned eighteen when he fell in love with a beautiful Lebanese girl by the name of Salma Karamay. This love both tragic and exalting had transformed his youth to the profound maturity of a sage and a mystic, to whom he would be wedded the rest of his life. Lebanon, in those days, was not only subjugated by the tyranny of the Turks, but crushed by the greed and corruption of the church and clergy. Under such conditions, a young man like Khalil Gibran, drunk by the wine of his first love and the purity of his soul his only wealth had no chance to win the hand of Salma in marriage. She was the daughter of a wealthy merchant, and her fate was sealed by the power and conceit of a Bishop, who had chosen her to be married to his own nephew. So his First Love Supreme was lost to the nephew of a rapacious Bishop.

Khalil Gibran was never to forget the grief, agony and sweetness of that first love his entire life. Salma was married to Mansour Bey, who had no interest in her, but in her inheritance. She was married to Misery, and he exiled from the Paradise of happiness, but they had chosen a place of rendezvous in one abandoned temple with the statues of Jesus and Mary on one side and of Ishthar on the other. There, they would sit for hours, sharing their sorrows, yet enveloped in bliss in togetherness. This bliss was not to last long; Salma had conceived, and upon the birth of her son, both the son and the mother died.

Inconsolable and grief-stricken, Khalil Gibran had bid farewell to Lebanon, journeying to Syria, Palestine, Greece, Rome, and Spain. His father had accompanied him on these tours and wanderings, and had left him in Paris for further studies. Soon, he was back in Boston, his grief buried deep inside him, and his heart longing for the Touch of the Divine. During that brief period of Anguish and Awakening, he was moved more by the sufferings of the others, than by his own, dissolving his own grief in words and colors, which could only be uttered or painted by the Light of Inspiration.

The Light of Inspiration and his longing to seek the Beloved were Khalil Gibran's only companions, leading him through the marshes of more tragedies, and lending him the sight of Vision and Prophecy. He had accumulated a wealth of writings and paintings from the profound deeps in his own inner being, which didn't earn him riches, but great admiration from the audience in Lebanon and America. The shadow of tragedy didn't leave him, for soon his mother succumbed to death by cancer, claiming two more victims, his brother Peter and his sister Sultana of tuberculosis.

Khalil Gibran, by then, had reached the depths of mysticism, his character one of gentle melancholy, and pressed by the soul-searching need for knowledge to improve the lot of his countrymen burdened with despair and oppression. During that time, the poet and artist in him reached to the greatest heights, singing the Elysian beauty of youth and death, and his brush revealing the man's inhumanity to man. His famous painting is the one with an eye in its palm, representing the Phoenician Goddess, Tanit.

What I say now with one heart, will be said tomorrow with many hearts.

With this prophetic statement, Khalil Gibran used his pen as a sword against the religious injustice of the church and his countrymen. He wrote about the degradation of society throughout the East, touching about the theme of universal love and brotherhood.

How can existence on earth be endured when love departs, friendship withers… Khalil Gibran wrote, aiming to promote charity, kindness and spiritual awareness. Dreaming of utopia, full of love and eternal happiness, he contracted another friendship with a Lebanese woman who had migrated to Egypt. May Zaideh was her name, and she was a great admirer of his works. This friendship lasted on paper for nineteen years until his death, only through correspondence, and they never met each other in person. Another close friend of Khalil Gibran was Barbara Young, who became his secretary and remained so for the last seven years of his life until his death in New York. Khalil Gibran died in Vincent Hospital due to the Cirrhosis of the liver with incipient tuberculosis in one of his lungs. After some months, his remains from Boston were transferred to Lebanon, and laid in the chapel of Mar Sarkis. It was an old monastery carved in a rock near Bsharri.

Khalil Gibran's thoughts about his first love:

Salma was the one who taught me to worship beauty by the example of her own beauty and revealed to me the secret of love by her affection. She was the one who first sang to me the poetry of real life.

In every young man's life there is Salma who appears to him suddenly while in the spring of life and transforms his solitude into happy moments and fills the silence of his nights with music.

The first Eve led Adam out of Paradise by her own will, while Salma made me enter willingly into the paradise of pure love and virtue by her love and sweetness. But what happened to the first man also happened to me. And the fiery sword which chased Adam out of Paradise was like the one which frightened me by its glittering edge and forced me away from the paradise of my love without having disobeyed any order or tasted the fruit of the forbidden tree.

After the death of Salma, Khalil Gibran writes in memory of his love, as if still mourning at her grave:

Oh friends of my youth who are scattered in the city of Beirut, when you pass by that cemetery near the pine forest, enter it silently and walk slowly so the tramping of your feet will not disturb the slumber of the dead, and stop humbly by Salma's tomb and greet the earth that embraces her corpse and mention my name with a deep sigh and say to yourself:

Here all the hopes of Gibran, who is living as a prisoner of love beyond the seas, were buried. On this spot, he lost his happiness, drained his tears, and forgot his smile.

Khalil Gibran is the author of many great works, but his most famous ones are, The Prophet, and Broken Wings. He is a great artist, too; most of his paintings are on display at the museum in Lebanon.

Khalil Gibran
Artist and Mystic of the Holy Cedars

Only those return to Eternity
Who on earth seek out Eternity

The seed which
The ripe date contains in its
Heart is the secret of the palm

Tree from the beginning of all
Creation

In the wild there is no Credo
Nor a hideous disbelief
Song-birds never are assertive
Of the Truth, the Bliss, or Grief

To Nature all are alive and all are
Free, The earthly glory of man is an
Empty dream, vanishing with the bubbles
In the rocky stream

Man's will is a floating shadow
In the mind he conceives
And the rights of mankind pass and
Perish like the autumn leaves

During the ebb, I wrote a line upon the sand
Committing to it all that is in my soul and mind
I returned at the tide to read it and to ponder upon it
I found naught upon the seashore but my ignorance

The power to Love
Is God's greatest gift to man
For it never will be taken from the
Blessed one who loves
Love lies in the soul alone
Not in the body, and like wine
Should stimulate our better self
To welcome gifts of Love Divine

Circumstance drives us on
In narrow paths by Kismet hewn
For fate has ways we cannot change
While weakness preys upon our will

We bolster with excuse the self
And help that fate ourselves to kill

I sought happiness in my solitude, and
As I drew close to her I heard my soul
Whisper into my heart, saying
'The happiness you seek is a virgin
Born and reared in the depths of each heart
And she emerges not from her birthplace'
And when I opened my heart to find her
I discovered in its domain only her
Mirror and her cradle and her raiment
And happiness was not there

Happiness is a myth we seek
If manifested surely irks
Like river speeding to the plain
On its arrival slows and murks
For man is happy only in
His aspiration to the heights
When he attains his goal, he cools
And longs for other distant flights
Happiness on earth is but a fleet
Passing ghost, which man craves
At any cost in gold or time, and
When the phantom becomes reality
Man soon wearies of it

Hear us, Oh Liberty
Bring mercy, Oh Daughter of Athens
Rescue us, Oh Sister of Rome
Advise us, Oh Companion of Moses
Help us, Oh Beloved of Muhammed
Teach us, Oh Bride of Jesus
Strengthen our hearts so we may live
Or harden our enemies so we may perish

And live in peace eternally

The Prophet arrives
Veiled in the cloak of future thought
'Mid people hid in ancient garb
Who could not see the gift he brought
He is a stranger to this life
Stranger to those who praise or blame
For he upholds the Torch of Truth
Although devoured by the flame'

Religion is a well-tilled field
Planted and watered by desire
Of one who longed for Paradise
Of one who dreaded Hell and Fire
Aye, were it but not for reckoning
At Resurrection, they had not
Worshipped God, nor did repent
Except to gain a better lot
As though religion were a phase
Of commerce in their daily trade
Should they neglect it, they would lose
Or persevering would be paid

Learning follows various roads
We note the start but not the end
For Time and Fate must rule the course
While we see not beyond the bend
The best knowledge is a dream
The gainer holds steadfast, uncowed
By ridicule, and moved serene
Despised and lowly in the crowd

Justice on earth would cause the Jinn
To cry at the misuse of the word
And were the dead to witness it

They'd mock at the fairness in this world
Yea, death and prison we mete out
To small offenders of the laws
While honor, wealth and full respect
On greater pirates we bestow
To steal a flower we call mean
To rob a field is chivalry
Who kills the body must die
Who kills the spirit he goes free

Oh, comrades of my youth
I appeal to you in the name of those virgins
Whom your hearts have loved
To lay a wreath of flowers
On the forsaken tomb of my beloved
For the flowers you lay on Salma's tomb
Are like falling drops of dew
From the eyes of dawn
On the leaves of a
Withering Rose

Death on earth, to son of earth
Is final, but to him who is
Ethereal, it is but a start
Of triumph certain to be his
If one embraces dawn in dreams
He is immortal, should he sleep
His long night through, he surely fades
Into a sea of slumber deep
For he who closely hugs the ground
When wide awake will crawl endlessly
And death, like sea, who braves it light
Will cross it, Weighted will descend

The gentleness of some is like
A polished shell with silky feel

Lacking the precious pearl within
Oblivious to the brother's weal
When you shall meet one who is strong
And gentle too, pray feast your eyes
For he is glorious to behold
The blind can see his qualities

O, Mist, my sister, my sister, Mist
I am one with you now
No longer am I self
The walls have fallen
And the chains have broken
I rise to you, a mist
And together we shall float upon the sea until
Life's second day
When dawn shall lay you, dewdrops in
A garden
And me a babe upon the breast of a woman

Feed the lamp with oil and let it not dim, and
Place it by you, so I can read with tears what
Your life with me has written upon your face
Bring autumn's wine, let us drink and sing the
Song of remembrance to spring's carefree sowing
And summer's watchful tending
And autumn's reward in harvest
Come close to me, oh beloved of my soul
The fire is cooling and fleeing under the ashes
Embrace me, for I feel loneliness, the lamp is
Dim, and the wine which we pressed is closing
Our eyes
Let us look upon each other before
They are shut

SONG OF LOVE

I Am the lover's eyes, and the spirit's
Wine, and the heart's nourishment
I am a rose, my heart opens at dawn and
The virgin kisses me and places me
Upon her breast
I am the house of true fortune, and the
Origin of pleasure, and the beginning
Of peace and tranquility, I am the gentle
Smile upon the lips of beauty, when youth
Overtakes me he forgets his toil, and his
Whole life becomes reality of sweet dreams
I am the poet's elation
And the artist's revelation
And the musician's inspiration
I am a sacred shrine in the heart of a
Child, adored by a merciful mother
I appear to a heart's cry, I shun a demand
My fullness pursues the heart's desire
It shuns the empty claim of the voice
I appeared to Adam through Eve
And exile was his lot
Yet I revealed myself to Solomon, and
He drew wisdom from my presence
I smiled at Helena and she destroyed Tarwada
Yet I crowned Cleopatra and peace dominated
The Valley of the Nile
I am like the ages—building today
And destroying tomorrow
I am like a god, who creates and ruins
I am sweeter than a violet's sigh
I am more violent than a raging tempest
Gifts alone do not entice me
Parting does not discourage me
Poverty does not chase me

Jealousy does not prove my awareness
Madness does not evidence my presence
Oh, seekers, I am Truth, beseeching Truth
And your Truth in seeking and receiving
And protecting me shall determine my
Behavior

SONG OF MAN

I was here from the moment of the
Beginning, and here I am still, and
I shall remain here until the end
Of the world, for there is no
Ending to my grief-stricken being
I roamed the infinite sky, and
Soared the ideal world, and
Floated through the firmament, but
Here I am, prisoner of measurement
I heard the teaching of Confucius
I listened to Brahma's wisdom
I sat by Buddha under the Tree of Knowledge
Yet here am I, existing with ignorance
And heresy
I was on Sinai when Jehovah approached Moses
I saw the Nazarene's miracles at Jordan
I was in Medina when Mohammed visited
Yet here I am, prisoner of bewilderment
Then I witnessed the might of Babylon
I learned the glory of Egypt
I viewed the warring greatness of Rome
Yet my earlier teachings showed the
Weakness and sorrow of those achievements
I conversed with the magicians of Ain Dour
I debated with the priests of Assyria
I gleaned depth from the prophets of Palestine
Yet I am still seeking the truth

I gathered wisdom from quiet India
I probed the antiquity of Arabia
I heard all that can be heard
Yet my heart is deaf and blind
I suffered at the hands of despotic rulers
I suffered slavery under insane invaders
I suffered hunger imposed by tyranny
Yet, I still possess some inner power
With which I struggle to greet each day
My mind is filled, but my heart is empty
My body is old, but my heart is an infant
Perhaps in youth my heart will grow, but I
Pray to grow old and reach the moment of
My return to God, only then will my heart fill
I was here from the moment of the
Beginning, and here I am still and
I shall remain here until the end
Of the world, for there is no
Ending to my grief-stricken being

A LOVER'S CALL

Where are you, my beloved
Are you in that little Paradise
Watering the flowers, who look upon you
As infants look upon the breasts of their mothers
Or are you in your chamber where the shrine of Virtue
Has been placed in your honor, and upon which
You offer my heart and soul as sacrifice
Or amongst the books, seeking human knowledge
While you are replete with heavenly wisdom
Oh companion of my soul, where are you
Are you praying in the temple
Or calling Nature in the Field
Haven of your dreams
Are you in the huts of the poor, consoling

The broken-hearted with the sweetness of your soul
And filling their hands with your bounty
You are God's spirit everywhere
You are stronger than the ages
Do you have memory of the day we met
When the halo of your spirit surrounded us
And the angels of love floated about
Singing the praise of the soul's deeds
Do you recollect our sitting in the shade of the branches
Sheltering ourselves from Humanity
As the ribs protect the divine secret of the heart from injury
Remember you the trails and forest we walked
With hands joined, and our heads leaning against each other
As if we were hiding ourselves within ourselves
Recall you the hour I bade you farewell
And the Mariamite kiss you placed on my lips
That kiss taught me that joining of lips in Love
Reveals heavenly secrets which the tongue cannot utter
That kiss was an introduction to a great sigh
Like the Almighty's breath that turned earth into man
That sigh led my way into the spiritual world
Announcing the glory of my soul, and there
It shall perpetuate until again we meet
I remember when you kissed me and kissed me
With tears coursing your cheeks, and you said
'Earthly bodies must often separate for earthly purpose
And must live apart impelled by worldly intent
But the spirit remains joined safely in the hands of Love
Until death arrives and takes joined souls to God
Go, my beloved, Love has chosen you her delegate
Obey her, for she is Beauty who offers to her follower
The cup of the sweetness of life
As for my own empty arms, your love shall remain
My comforting groom
Your memory, my eternal wedding'
Where are you now, my other self

Are you awake in the silence of the night
Let the clean breeze convey to you
My heart's every beat and affection
Are you fondling my face in your memory
That image is no longer my own
For sorrow has dropped its shadow
On my happy countenance of the past
Sobs have withered my eyes, which reflected your beauty
And dried my lips which you sweetened with kisses
Where are you, my beloved, do you hear my weeping
From beyond the ocean, do you understand my need
Do you know the greatness of my patience
Is there any spirit in the air capable of conveying
To you the breath of this dying youth
Is there any secret communication between angels
That will carry to You my complaint
Where are you, my beautiful star, the obscurity of life
Has cast me upon its bosom, sorrow has conquered me
Sail your smile into the air, it will reach and enliven me
Breathe your fragrance into the air, it will sustain me
Where are you, my beloved
Oh, how great is Love
And how little am I

Fare you well, people of Orphalese
This day has ended
Forget not that I shall come back to you
A little while, and my longing shall
Gather dust and foam for another body
A little while, a moment of rest upon
The wind, and another woman shall
Bear me

CHAPTER EIGHT

Umar Ibn al-Farid
Born in Egypt 1181-1235

Once the doors of the heart are open
The feeling of humility awakens
Finding oneself face to face
With the Divine Presence
The living God within   Hidayat Inayat Khan

Sufi, wisdom, religion, mysticism and spirituality, in the words of Hidayat Khan, present a clear picture of the Quest Divine in living the life of Love and Purity.

The message of Love, Beauty and Harmony is like a stream flowing onwards along the riverside of our daily lives, and this stream is in movement. A movement of Spiritual Liberty, and movement of Purity and Wisdom, all of which is understood by the word SUFI. Wisdom is the art of being responsive to the opinions of others and tolerant of their pre-conceived ideas, while preserving one's own understanding from the limitations of dogma. Religion is the path of liberation from the captivity of that illusion which arises when one assumes a duality in the unity of love, human and divine. Mysticism is an inner awakening to the reality of the un-definable, which is experienced when the voice of the heart cries aloud: This is not my body, this is the temple of God! Spirituality is the process of clearing away all aspects of self-assertion while at the same time searching for the divine impulse within oneself, which is the source and goal of all creation.

Sufi means Love, and Creation is the manifestation of God's Love for Man and World. A Sufi understands this Love through the Circle of Knowledge in his own Being, where he has dared enter to see the Face of the Beloved. This Beloved becomes the Sufi's Guide, dissolving the veils of Illusion, and revealing a world all Perfect and Beautiful. While we see pain, misery, ugliness and a world rigged with hatred, prejudice, violence, just to name a few of the evils of our time in timelessness, a Sufi sees nothing but Perfection in all its Entirety, where *evils* as the veils of illusions have fallen, only the Love of the Beloved shines forth as the Light of Oneness, the Divine Source, to Whom We All Return, healed and purified of all our illusions earthly or divine. Only the True Seekers, the Lovers of the Beloved, burning with the Flame of Longing, courting humility and surrender on the Way reach that Inner Circle of Love. And when they come out of that Holy Abode, nothing is left of them but the Light of Love for All to melt the curtains of Illusion which we perceive as reality in health and sickness, in joy and sorrow, in life and death. The poetry of divine inspiration, in turn, becomes our guide to see the palace of duality crumbling before our very eyes in realms both Sufic and Mystic.

Ibn al-Farid's life is revealed to the world through his famous odes, Wine Ode and The Sufi Way. The details about his personal life are scant, with the exception of what his grandson has written about his character and mystical experiences, much in the likeness of the saints who wear their death shroud woven in Visions and Miracles. Ibn al-Farid was born in Egypt, probably married to an Egyptian girl, and had sons and daughters. He spent most of his life in Cairo where he taught Hadith and poetry. He also traveled to Mecca, where he spent almost thirteen years, visiting holy places and pressed by a longing to be united with the Beloved. He had attained that Union long before he died inside the lonesome sanctuary of Azhar mosque, his odes staying behind, as true witnesses to his Bliss supreme and Beloved sublime!

His Love for God and poetry was so intense that upon hearing love poems or Quranic verses, he would be driven into ecstasy, or tear his clothes and run naked on the streets. After that, the fountain of his Passion and Inspiration would break loose, and he would sing of the love human and love divine. The wine in his poems is not the earthly drink, but the emblem of lost union with the Beloved, the lost Paradise. Wine is the mystical substance, and poetry sweet water of love, which unites the Lover with the Beloved. Drinking of this wine is for the heart and the spirit, not for the body. This wine is the life-blood of the Lover who can taste its sweetness only after journeying through the valleys of discipline, deprivation and transformation, finally reaching the Garden of Union to receive this Gift of Wine. Annihilation of the ego and selfishness is the Sufi's ascent to the divine Beloved. Wine becomes the Beloved, and

Beloved is Her, whom he calls My All. In his odes, he becomes the spiritual guide, exploring the life within, calling his listeners to set out on a pilgrimage which would show them the Path to God. His God is gender-free, sometimes, it's a beautiful girl, and other times, he the Beloved. He tells his audience, if one does not love passionately, one possibly cannot travel the Sufi Way.

Moses and Khidr story:

As a spiritual guide, Ibn al-Farid points out the mists of ignorance which cloud our mortal senses and sight, and recounts this story. This is the story of a mystical transformation, where Moses encounters a mysterious stranger, later identified in Islamic tradition as the prophet Khidr, the Invisible Guide. Moses meets Khidr in his wanderings, pleading with him to take him along wherever he is going. Khidr agrees reluctantly, requesting in return that Moses would not ask any questions. Moses agrees, but can't keep quiet since Khidr gets involved in tragic events on the way without appearing to be affected in the least. Khidr kills a youth at one stage on their journey, and then repairs the broken wall of an inhospitable house without any reason. Further down the way, Khidr damages a perfectly good boat, as if moved by his own silent whim or caprice. When plied with questions by Moses, he explains that these matters are not as they appear to be on the surface. The slain youth would have grown to be a disgrace to his parents, and God would grant them another offspring of worthy qualities. The wall had to be repaired, because it contained a hidden treasure belonging to two orphans, who would claim it when they are of age. The boat belonged to the poor people for their livelihood, but a cruel king was on his way to seize all good boats, and it had to be damaged so that the king would not take it, which the poor people could repair later. Khidr had the knowledge of the hidden dimensions of reality, so he could act according to the laws of nature, which appeared wrong to the less perceptive, but fitted perfectly in the whole scheme of Perfect Reality.

There is Khidr in everyone's psyche in the odes of Ibn al-Farid, who can lift the veils of ignorance, if one approaches him with utmost trust and silence in one's own soul. The Poem of the Sufi Way is a microcosm of Islamic tradition, and Ibn al-Farid uses the key themes directly from the Quran and Hadith. His mystical aim *the passing away* of the human self is in mystical union with the divine. A few of the themes in his odes are borrowed from the poetic verses of the Quran, such as:

To God belongs the east and west, wherever you turn, there is the face of God. 2:115

If your servant inquire of you concerning Me. Lo, I am near. 2:186

We are nearer to human beings than his jugular vein. 50:16

God loves those who depend upon Him completely. 3:159

O self at peace, return to your Lord, contended and pleasing. Enter among my servants and enter my garden. 89:27-30

Briefly, Ibn al-Farid bears witness to the transformative power of love, while urging his listeners, both the Sufi devotees of the past and ultimately, those of us in the present, to undertake a journey of personal exploration and mystical discovery.

Ibn al-Farid is buried in the Qarafah cemetery in Cairo below the Azhar mosque, near Moses' Place of Prostration at the foot of Mt. Muquattam

Ibn al-Farid
Sufi Poet in Arabic

If not for you, I would not know love
If not for love, I would not know you

For the secret of *Indeed, Yes!*
Is the mirror of God's unveiling
And the meaning of union is confirmed
With the denial of *with-ness*

In memory of the beloved
We drank a wine
We were drunk with it
Before creation of the vine

I imagined sobriety
As my pedigree, and intoxication
My ascent to her, with effacement
My Lote tree's end in space
But when I cleared the clouds away
I found myself up and awake
While my inner spring
Refreshed my eyes
And from my drunken poverty
I recovered, grew rich
In my second separation
Union like oneness to me

The tongues of all beings
If you listen close
Witness with eloquence
To my unity
While about my union
A tradition has come
Its transmission clear
Without doubt
Declaring true love
For those who draw near Him
By willing devotions
Or those decreed
The point of its teaching
Is clear
As noonday light
I am his ear…

It is love, so guard your heart
Passion is not easy
Wasted by it, would you choose it
If you had reason
Live free of love

For love's ease is hard
It begins in sickness
And ends in death
But to me, death in love
By drowning desire
Is life revived
By my beloved
I have warned you
Knowing passion and my enemy
So choose for yourself
What is sweet
But if you want to live well
Then die love's martyr
And if not, well
Love has its worthy ones
Not to die in love
Is not to live by love
Before you harvest honey
You must surely face the bees

Though he be absent from me
Every grasping sense sees him
In every subtle sense
Lovely and pure
In the melody
Of the lyre and gentle flute
When they embrace
In trilling notes of song
In the meadows
Of the forest gazelle
In twilight's cool
And daybreak's glow
Where the mist
Falls from clouds
On a blossoming carpet
Woven from flowers

Where the zephyr
Sweeps its skirts
Gliding to me at dawn
The sweetest scent
And in my kissing
The cup's lip
Sipping wine drops
In pure pleasure
I never knew exile
When he was with me
And wherever we were
My mind was at quiet rest

When a devotee falls down
Before an idol temple's stones
Do not transgress
And censure from bigotry
For many of those free
From the idol's shame
Are bound secretly within
To worship cash and coin
My warning has reached
Those who heed
And by me, absolution has arisen
For all who broke away
The eyes of every faith
Have never strayed
Nor did the thoughts of any creed
Ever swerve aside
One dazed in desire for the sun
Is not deranged
For it shines from the light
Of my blazing splendor, unveiled
And when the Magi worship the fire
That, tradition tells
Has been burning bright

For a thousand years
They aim only for me
Though they do not show
A firm resolve
As they seek another

I raised the screen from my soul
By lifting up the veil
And so it answered my question
I had rubbed the rust of my attributes
From the mirror of my being
And it was encircled
With my beaming rays
And I summoned me to witness me
Since no other existed
In my witness
To rival me
My mentioning my name
Made me hear it in my recollection
As my soul, negating sense
Said my name and listened
I hugged myself
But not by wrapping arms around my ribs
That I might embrace
My identity
I inhaled my spirit
While the air of my breath
Perfumed scattered ambergris
With fragrance

So there is no spreading gloom or darkness
There is no wrong to fear
As the grace of my light
Puts out the fire of my wrath
And there is no time
Save where time does not count

The existence of my being
By the cycle of the moon
Yet the captive of time's constraints
Will never see
What is beyond this cell
In the garden of forever
The celestial spheres turn on me
So marvel at the pole of their turning
A central point
That circles them all
There is no axis before me
To succeed based on the three
The pole arises from the pegs
Fastened among my substitutes
So do not cross my straight line
For in the corners
Are hidden things
Seize your best chance now
From me, the seed of love
Appeared in me
And for me, the breast of union
Flowed from me with milk

By union
Noah rose above the flood
And saved his folk
Who sought refuge in the ark
The deluge receded
In answer to his prayer
And he sailed straight to Mt Judi
And the ark settled there
With the wind's back
Bearing up his carpet
Solomon and his armies, too
Swept across the earth's expanse
And before the blink of an eye

The throne of queen Bilqis
Was brought to him easily
From Sheba
Abraham quelled the fire of his foe
And from his light
The flames became a meadow
In a garden
And when he summoned birds
From each mountaintop
They came without complaint
Though they had been killed and quartered
Moses threw down his staff
Which swallowed up
The terrors of sorcery
Preying on his soul
And from his striking a stone
Springs burst out
Streaming continuously
Running to the sea
When the messenger
Cast Joseph's shirt
Over Jacob's face
With news of his son's return
Jacob saw Joseph from afar
With eyes long blind
From weeping
Longing for him
Among the people of Israel
A table spread for the feast
Came down from heaven
To Jesus
He made the blind see
Restored the leper's health
And with a breath, he turned dead clay
Into a breathing bird
With God's permission

My finely forged words
Have revealed to you the secret
Within actions without
And the secrets of all of them before
Were brought and bestowed on us
By him who was their seal
In prophecy's due time

For my soul had fought hard
And died a martyr on its path
It gained glad tidings
When it paid its price in full
Then, due to my union, my soul soared with me
Beyond the eternal life of its heaven
As I was not inclined to linger
On the earth of my deputy
How could I fall under the reign
Of those over whom I rule
The keepers of my kingdom
My followers, my troops, and partisans
For there is no heavenly sphere
Without an angel within
Giving guidance by my will
From the light of my inner being
And there is no earthly clime
Without a drop falling there
Causing clouds to flow with rain
From the flow of my outer form
Compared to my dawn
The long day's light is my flash
Next to my drinking place
The wide ocean is a drop
So the whole of me
Faces and seeks my all
While part of me with bridle and reins
Draws my other part

One who was above below
While above was below him
Every direction submitted
To his guiding countenance
This earth's below is ether above
Because what I split is closed
Though splitting the closure
Is my obvious way
There is no ambiguity
Union is the source of certainty
There is no where
As space only separates
There is no number
For counting cuts like the blade edge
Nor is there time since limit
Is a timekeeper's idolatry
There is no equal in this world or the next
Who could decree to raze what I raised up
Or command to carry out
The decree of my command
There is no rival in either place
And due to harmony
You will not see disparity
In humanity's creation
From me, there appeared to me
What I donned as my disguise from me
And I returned to me
My wandering apparitions

My spirit soared past the fate
Opening to beyond my union
Where there is no veil
In communion
One who follows after me
Choosing his gaze as his goal like me
Let him ride for it

With a true resolve
For into how many dark depths
Did I dive before I passed through
Where the poor ascetic seeking fortune
Never even wet his lips
In the mirror of my words, I will show you
The door if you are determined
So attend to what I bestow
Upon the ear of insight
Out of jealousy, I cast out
My words from all statements
My share
Of every act and action
My regard for the fine reward of works
And my guarding mystic states
From the disgrace
Of ostentation
My preaching with sincere intent
The devotee's denial and abstinence
And my casting out of all concern
For every casting out
So my heart is a holy house
In which I dwell
Before it, rising out of it
My attributes appear from my veiling
My right hand is a corner there
Kissed within me, and by wise decree
My kiss comes to my mouth
From my niche for prayer
Mysteriously my turning
Is really around me
And I am toward myself
From my Safa to my Marwah
In a sanctuary within
My appearance is safe
But around it my neighbors

Risk being snatched away
By fasting my soul alone
From all others was purified
And gave as alms
The grace flowing from me
And my existence
Bent double in my witnessing
Became straight and single in my union
The night journey of my inner heart
From privileged truth to me
Is like my course
Among the common cares of law

Divinity did not distract me
From the rules of my appearance
Nor did human nature lead me to forget
Where my wisdom was manifest
So from me the covenants
Were bound to the soul
And from me the limits
Were set upon the senses
For an apostle had come
To me from myself
Troubled by my wanton ways
Caring and compassionate toward me
Thus from myself
I passed my decree upon my soul
When it took charge of affairs
It never turned back
From the age of my covenant
Before the era of my elements
Before my mission
Warning of resurrection time
I was a messenger
Sent to me, from me
And by my signs

My being was led to me
By right of its purchase
I transferred the soul
From its earthly possession
To the Garden's dominion

I am amazed by the drunkenness of mine
One without wine
As I am moved within my hidden heart
By rapture arising from me
So my heart dances
And my trembling limbs clap like a chanter
With my spirit
As my singing girl
My soul continued
To be nourished by desires
As it effaced the frail faculties
And grew in strength
I found all existing things
Allied to help there
Though, in fact, the aid
Was my own assistance from me
That every member might
Unite all of me to her
That every root of hair
Could contain my union
That any guise of estrangement
Might be stripped away between us
Though I never found it to be
Other than my intimacy
Now push aside your studies and note
How the senses convey to the soul
By the inspiration of intuition
What she has brought to light
The north wind guides
Her memory to my spirit

Whenever it comes from her by night
Rising up at dawn
And my ear is pleased
When her memory is roused at noon
By dusky doves on branches
Warbling and gently cooing
My eye is blessed
When a lightning flash
Relays to it from her
Thought of her in the evening
And I taste the touch
Her memory in vessels of wine
When, at night
They come round to me
Thus my heart reveals to me
Her memory within
By what the sense-messengers
Delivered from without
One who chants her name brings me
To the gathering of union
Whereby by listening, I witness her
With my all
Then my spirit soars toward heaven
To the gathering of union
While this created body turns back
Toward my earthly friends with affection

All that you witness
Is the act of one
Alone within
The cloistering veils
But when he removes the screen
You see none but him
No doubt lingers
About the shapes and forms
And you realize

When the truth is shown
That by his light you were guided
To his actions in the shadows

CHAPTER NINE

Kabir 1440-1518   **Rabindranath Tagore 1861-1941**
Born in Banares, North India   Born in Calcutta, India

Take our salutations, Lord, from every quarter
 Infinite of might and boundless in your glory
  You are all that is, since everywhere we find you
Bhagavad-Gita

The Indian Sufis and Mystics are no different than any other Sufis and Mystics of the World. They, too, practice the religion of the heart, and dancing the dance of love and harmony. In conformity with their own time and age, they venture forth to right the wrongs of society with the Pen of Inspiration, or simply toss their wisdom to the winds; hoping that mankind might catch a few pearls of *Knowledge* Divine, or Divinity in *Understanding*.

It stirs and it stirs not, it is far, and likewise near
It is inside of all this, and it is outside of all this
He moves and he moves not, He is far, and He is near
He is within all, and He is outside all

This verse from the Isa Upanishads, from one of the holy books of the Hindus sums up the quests of the Indian Mystics to seek their Beloved. The journey is long and arduous, but when the Seeker and the Sought are united in Love, all time, forms and names dissolve to nothingness. The Adorer and the Adored are One, kindled with the Divine Flame of Perception to serve mankind. And the only way they know to render this service to mankind is through the poetry of their expression. Mystics of the East have imbibed the rich culture of their homeland with insatiable thirst and passion for knowledge, journeying through turbulent times in history, before embarking on the Journey to seek the Beloved whom no history or thought can define, the Unfathomable. *Formless in timelessness!* One can journey with them to fathom the Unfathomable.

Kabir is not only a Sufi, but a satirist and reformer, singing in ecstasy the songs of beauty and harmony, his wit is most profound when chiseling away the layers of hypocrisy from the teachings of the pundits and the mullahs.

Kabir's family belonged to a caste of weavers, their socioeconomic status low, as conjectured, though we know very little about his life. His family had converted to Islam a century or two ago before he was born, but in predominantly Hindu India, Kabir was exposed to both the cultures and religions of the Hindus and the Muslims.

Kabir is a Muslim name, but his approach to the Truth or Beloved reveals more influence of Hindu and Buddhist traditions than of Islam. He prefers the name of Ram for God, in conformity with the legend that he tricked a Brahmin guru by the name of Ramanandar into accepting him as his student. It is assumed that he was illiterate, imparting his genius to the world through oral song and poetry.

In the sixteenth century, the influence of nascent religion of the Sikhs was expanding into various sects in different parts of the country. Sikh Panth in the Punjab; Dadu Panth in Rajasthan and Kabir Panth in Bihar and Uttar Pradesh. In the holy book of the Sikhs, many of Kabir's verses are quoted.

Many legends are woven around Kabir's life, but the most famous one is at his death. After his death, when Kabir's body was prepared for its final internment, both Hindus and Muslims lined up on each side of his bier, each faction demanding that he should be buried according to their own religious rites. Hindus wanted to cremate his body, the Muslims wanted to bury it in the grave, even swords were drawn to settle the issue. But just before the bloody confrontation could commence, someone yanked the burial shroud off from the body of the deceased. Amidst the waves of shock and stunned silence, no one could see the corpse of Kabir, but a pile of fresh roses. So both Hindus and Muslims divided those flowers, Hindus committing them to the holy flames as the rite of cremation, and the Muslims burying them under earth with all reverence.

Kabir
Songs of the Indian Sufi

Wherever I look
Only this, only this
The diamond pierced
My ruby heart

The Hindu says Ram is the Beloved
The Turk says Rahim
Then they kill each other
Nobody knows the secret

Dance done without feet
Tune played without hands
Praises sung without tongue
Singer without shape or form
The true teacher reveals
Of the source-less state, what to say
No town, nowhere to stay
Seen without a trace
What do you call that place
A sweet word is a healing herb
A bitter word is an arrow
Entering by the door of the ear
It tears through the whole body

A gown of love-silk
Put it on, Kabir
And dance
They shine with beauty
Who speak truth
With mind and body

Within the heart a mirror
But no face shows

You'll see the face when the heart's
Double-ness goes

Color is born of color
I see all colors one
What color is a living creature
Solve it if you can

The road the pundits took
Crowds took
Ram's pass is a high one
Kabir keeps climbing

No one knows the secret of the weaver
Who spread his warp through the universe
He dug two ditches, sky and earth
Made two spools, sun and moon
Filled his shuttle with a thousand threads
And weaves till today, a difficult length
Kabir says, they're joined by actions
Good threads and bad
That Fellow weaves both

Moving within limits: man
Moving without limits: saint
Dropping both limits and no-limits
Unfathomable thought

The worldling ponders
Domestic life or yoga
He loses his chances
While others grow conscious
It's the kind of speech
No eye can see
Kabir says, listen
To the word spoken

In every body

I looked and looked—astonishing
Only a rare one hears me sing
The earth shot backwards to the sky
An elephant fell in an ant's eye
Mountains flew without a breeze
Souls and creatures climbed the trees
In a dry lake, the waves lashed
Without water, water-birds splashed
Pundits sat and read the law
Babbled of what they never saw
Who understands Kabir's rhyme
Is a true saint to the end of time

It's not a wild beast, brother
Not a wild beast
But everyone eats
The meat
The beast is a whole world
Unimaginable
Tear open the belly
No liver or guts
It's this kind of meat, brother
Every minute sold
Bones and hooves on the dump
Fire and smoke
Won't eat it
No head, no horn
And where's a tail
All the pundits meet
And fight
Kabir sings a marriage song

Saints, if I speak
Who will believe it

If I lie it passes for truth
I glimpsed a jewel
Un-pierced and priceless
Without buyer or seller
Glistening, gleaming, it flashed
In my eyes, and filled
The ten directions
A touch of grace
From the guru
The invisible, the mark-less
Appeared
Simple meditation
Absolute stillness
Awakened, Simply
I am Ram

The musician plays a peerless instrument
With eight sky-mouths thundering
Only you are played, only you
Thunder, your hand alone
Runs up and down
In one sound thirty-six ragas, speaking
An endless word

The mouth a shaft
The ear a sounding gourd
The true teacher made the instrument
The tongue a string
The nose a peg
He rubs on the wax of Maya
Light bursts in the sky-temple
At a sudden
Reversal
Kabir says, clarity comes
When the musician lives
In your heart

Are you looking for Me
I am in the next seat
My shoulder is against yours
You will not find me in stupas
Not in Indian shrine rooms
Nor synagogues, nor in cathedrals
Not in masses, nor kirtans
Not in legs winding around your own neck
Nor in eating nothing but vegetables
When you really look for Me
You will see Me instantly
You will find Me in the tiniest house of time

Rabindranath Tagore came from a family of artists and musicians; they had great wealth and were well educated. Tagore was the fourteenth of the fifteenth children, endowed with creative and spiritual personality since childhood. During the years of his youth and education, his homeland India was going through the labor pains of birth, trying its utmost to free itself from the golden fetters of British Raj. Such were the times, splintered with conflict and violence, which made Tagore adopt a messianic role, the idealist in him proclaiming poet's religion to brave the storms of unrest and oppression. Since his youth, Tagore's need for the search for unity was being manifested in his lyrics and paintings. He had started writing in his teens, with a sense of the divine on paper and canvas both, his *need* and *spirituality* throbbing with the pulse of youth to sail beyond time and continents, and to discover the essence of Love in Unity. He was only fourteen when his mother died, and his poems were already appearing in a monthly journal owned by their family. The name of this journal was Bharati, and it would publish many more of his works during the trials and tribulations of his youth and manhood. He was a prolific writer and traveled extensively. His first visit to England was in Year 1877, and upon his return to India in 1883, was married to a girl much younger than him in conformity with the family tradition as arranged marriage. Two sons and two daughters were born out of this one and only marriage before his wife died in Year 1902. He loved his children; unfortunately, his eldest daughter and youngest son preceded him in death leaving him grief-stricken if not disconsolate. His social and personal life in cyclical patterns of hope and unpredictability had driven him closer to the spiritual world, where Mystery of the Mysterious could be felt much profoundly with all its joys and pains, too dear and too ineffable. His second visit to England was in Year 1909, and he had taken with him his book of songs, Gitanjali, translated by him and ready for publication. It proved to be an immediate success after its publication. His third visit to England was in Year 1912, and his first to America the same year. He received Noble Prize for literature in Year 1913, and was knighted in Year 1915, meeting with Gandhi the same year.

During his life and career, Tagore was hailed as the Shelley of Bengal, he himself always feeling alienated from the Mystic Abode of his Search, and hurled straight into the mouth of politics, feeling the labor pains of his Motherland India, and yearning to be the Son of Liberation. But his passionate yearnings with a mystic ideal seemed to slip away from him, as he tried to balance his quest for Love in the scale of Unity, the threat of war hovering over his shoulders as the hand of nemesis. With such a picture of disunity in his eyes and inside his head, when he died, he left the world a treasure of Mystic Pearls, and three thousand masterpieces painted with the Color of his own genius.

Rabindranath Tagore
A Mystic from Bengal

When one knows thee
Then alien there is none
Then no door is shut
Oh, grant me my prayer
That I may never lose the bliss
Of the touch of the one
In the play of many

What divine drink wouldst thou have, my God
From the overflowing cup of my life
My poet, is it thy delight

To see thy creation through my eyes
And to stand at the portals of my ears
Silently to listen to thine own eternal harmony
Thy world is weaving words in my mind
And thy joy is adding music to them
Thou givest thyself to me in love
And then feelest thine own entire
Sweetness in me

I am like the remnant of a cloud of autumn
Uselessly roaming in the sky
O my sun ever-glorious
Thy touch has not yet melted my vapor
Making me one with thy light
And thus I count months and years
Separated from thee
If this be thy wish and if this by thy play
Then take this fleeting emptiness of mine
Paint it with colors, gild it with gold
Float it on the wanton wind
And spread it in varied wonders
And again when it shall by thy wish
To end this play at night
I shall melt and vanish away in the dark
Or it may be in the smile of a white morning
In a coolness of purity transparent
Let only that little be left of me
Whereby I may name thee
My All
Let only that little be left of my will
Whereby I may feel thee on every side
And come to thee in everything
And offer to thee my love every moment
Let only that little be left of me
Whereby I may never hide thee
Let only that little of my fetters be left

Whereby I am bound by thy will
And thy promise is carried out in my life
And that is the fetter of thy love
The same stream of life that runs
Through my veins night and day
Runs through the world
And dances in rhythmic measures
It is the same life that shoots in joy
Through the dust of the earth
In numberless blades of grass
And breaks into tumultuous waves
Of leaves and flowers
It is the same life that is rocked
In the ocean-cradle of birth and of death
In ebb and in flow
I feel my limbs are made glorious
By the touch of this world of life
And my pride is from the life-throb of ages
Dancing in my blood this moment

Thou art the sky and thou art the nest as well
O thou beautiful, there in the nest it is thy love
That encloses the soul
With scents, sounds and colors
There comes the morning
With the golden basket in her right hand
Bearing the wreath of beauty
Silently to crown the earth
And there comes the evening
Over the lonely meadows deserted by herds
Through trackless paths, carrying cool draughts of peace
In her golden pitcher, form the western
Ocean of rest, but there
Where spreads the infinite sky
For the soul to take her flight in
Reigns the stainless white radiance

There is no day, nor night, nor form
Nor color, and never, never a word

That I should make much of myself
And turn it on all sides
Thus casting colored shadows
On thy radiance
Such is thy maya
Thou settest a barrier in thine own being
And then callest thy severed self in myriad notes
This thy self-separation had taken body in me
The poignant song is echoed through all the sky
In many colored tears and smiles, alarms and hopes
Waves rise up and sink again
Dreams break and form
In me is thy own defeat of self
This screen that thou hast raised is painted
With innumerable figures
With the brush of the night and the day
Behind it thy seat is woven
In wondrous mysteries of curves
Casting away all barren lines of straightness
The great pageant of me and thee
Has overspread the sky
With the tune of me and thee
All air is vibrant, and all ages pass
With the hiding and seeking of
Me and thee

Thou hast made me endless
Such is thy pleasure
This frail vessel thou emptiest
Again and again
And fillest it ever with fresh life
This little flute of a reed
Thou hast carried over hills and dales

And hast breathed through it
Melodies eternally new
At the immortal touch of thy hands
My little heart loses its limits in joy
And gives birth to utterance ineffable
Thy infinite gifts come to me
Only on these very small hands of mine
Ages pass, and still thou pourest
And still there is room to fill

When thou commandest me to sing
It seems that my heart would break with pride
And I look to thy face, and tears come to my eyes
All that is harsh and dissonant in my life
Melts into one sweet harmony
And my adoration spreads wings
Like a glad bird on its flight across the sea
I know thou takest pleasure in my singing
I know that only as a singer I come before thy presence
I touch by the edge of the far spreading wing of my song
Thy feet, which I could never aspire to reach
Drunk with the joy of singing
I forget myself and call thee friend
Who art my Lord
Life of my life
I shall ever try
To keep my body pure
Knowing that thy living touch
Is upon all my limbs
I shall ever try to keep
All untruths out of my thoughts
Knowing that thou art that truth
Which has kindled
The light of reason in my mind
I shall ever try to drive all evils away
From my heart, and keep my love in flower

Knowing that thou hast thy seat
In the innermost shrine of my heart
And it shall be my endeavor
To reveal thee in my actions
Knowing it is thy power
Gives me strength to act

My song has put off her adornments
She has no pride of dress and decoration
Ornaments would mar our union
They would come between me and thee
Their jingling would drown thy whispers
My poet's vanity dies in shame
Before thy sight, O master poet
I have sat down at thy feet
Only let me make my life
Simple and straight
Like a flute of reed for thee
To fill with music

Light, oh, where is the light
Kindle it with the burning fire of desire
There is the lamp but never one flicker of a flame
Is such thy fate, my heart
Ah, death were better by far for thee
Misery knocks at thy door, and her message is
That thy lord is wakeful, and he calls thee
To the love-tryst through the darkness of night
The sky is overcast with clouds
And the rain is ceaseless
I know not what this is that stirs in me
I know not its meaning
A moment's flash of lightning
Drags down a deeper gloom on my sight
And my heart gropes for the path
To where the music of the light calls me

Light, oh, where is the light
Kindle it with the burning fire of desire
It thunders and the wind rushes
Screaming through the void
The night is black as a black stone
Let not the hours pass by in the dark
Kindle the lamp of love with thy life

Deliverance is not for me in renunciation
I feel the embrace of freedom
In a thousand bonds of delight
Thou ever pourest for me the fresh draught
Of thy wine, of various colors and fragrance
Filling this earthen vessel to the brim
My world will light its hundred different lamps
With thy flame, and place them
Before the altar of thy temple
No, I will never shut the doors of my senses
The delights of sight and hearing
And touch will bear thy delight
Yes, all my illusions will burn
Into illumination of joy
And all my desires ripen
Into fruits of love

I seem to have loved you in numberless forms, numberless times
In life after life, in age after age forever
My spellbound heart has made and re-made the necklace of songs
That you take as a gift, wear round your neck in many forms
In life after life, in age after age forever
Whenever I hear old chronicles of love, its age-old pain
Its ancient tale of being apart or together
As I stare on and on into the past, in the end you emerge
Clad in the light of a pole-star, piercing the darkness of time
You become an image of what is remembered forever
You and I have floated here on the stream that brings from the fount

At the heart of time love of one for another
We have played alongside millions of lovers, shared in the same
Shy sweetness of meeting, the same distressful tears of farewell
Old love, but in shapes that renew and renew forever
Universal joy, universal sorrow, universal life
The memories of all loves merging with this one love of ours
And the songs of every poet past and forever

CHAPTER TEN

C. S. Lewis 1898-1963   **Saint Augustine 354-430**
Born in Belfast, Ireland   Born in Thagaste, North
Africa

As the flight of a river
That flows to the sea
My soul rushes over
In tumult to thee   E. G. Bulwer-Lytton

Sufis and Mystics are lovers, guides, friends and Seekers of beauty and Beloved. When the heart is pure, and the sight reflecting the purity of heart, one sees only beauty and perfection. This kind of beauty and perfection is the manifestation of one's own soul, the Abode of the Beloved. To reach this Holy Abode, one needs to learn the Music of Love, and tease the strings of Breath till the Harp of Life is in unison with the universe. Our breath is the only link to achieve Union with the Beloved. Sufis and Mystics follow this Breath like a shadow, holding the Flame of Desire as their eternal torch on their journey to the Source of Being. At every step, they encounter veils upon veils of illusions, tearing down each veil with the sword of Breath, and fighting the demons of fear and bewilderment in their quest to reach their destination. Finally, veils dissolve, illusions flee, self-annihilation rests on the baptismal waters of Knowledge, and one awakens to find out that one has journeyed not far, but within. Inside the confines of one's own ego, pride and Self, the subtle breath in its very essence of divine spark has the power and energy to guide one into the realms of spirituality. Inhaling through one nostril and exhaling through the other alternatively (like the channel of an inverted U) creates an even flow, which the Sufis and the Mystics master, concentrating on the very act of breathing to reach their goal of self-discipline, self-surrender, and ultimately self-Discovery through the very fires of love and longing.

The thought of mysticism has endless ability to capture the imagination. The immediate mental picture is of bliss, exalted thought, and insights denied not to those privileged to have the gift. Christian mysticism sees growth in spirituality as involving an ever deepening, personal relationship with God. The mystic, whose longing for a total bond with the Beloved, is not seeking nothingness, nor to 'find the God within.' His Lover is also a Person, albeit One Divine. Since the contemplation is a gift of grace from God Himself, the mystic remains fully, and, perhaps anxiously, aware that his/her own accomplishments and efforts cannot attain this union. (An excerpt from Cyberspace).

Since childhood, C. S. Lewis was endowed with a vivid and fertile imagination, which was greatly heightened by fantasy and fairy tales told to him by his mother. He was an avid reader, devouring Nesbit and Gulliver and Longfellow's saga of King Olaf, and falling in love with the magic and pagan myths of Norse legend. By the time he was twelve, those characters in the books had become so real that he could see them walking with him in the woods or gardens. He loved to contemplate, falling a little short of hallucination. *Once he was faintly alarmed*, he said, *when he thought he saw elves and dwarfs bounding past him in the woods.* As he grew older, his search for mysteries began in all earnest, but his childhood fantasies never left him.

Lewis went to a boarding school in Hertfordshire, England, exploring more authors and reading ravenously, two of his favorites, H. G. Wells and Rider Haggard. Then he moved to a preparatory school at Wyvern. Though he himself was a member of the Church of England, the orthodox views of the Church didn't suit him, and he told his friends he had ceased to be a Christian. At the age of twenty-seven, he began to teach English and Literature at Magdalen College. Soon, he met Tolkien at a meeting of the English faculty at Menton College, and they became great friends. During the long years of their friendship, both these men, inward bound for Truth, became the authors of great works. Lewis' great accomplishment was a seven-volume fantasy, The Chronicles of Narnia. Some see in this work a parallel to the warfare between God and Satan, but Lewis in his writings refutes such a suggestion, labeling his masterpieces simply as inspirational works.

The source of his inspiration was his Search for God, though he talked to that Source in angry, bitter words, since his imagination brought him closer to that Source than any saint or prophet. And yet, the mystic in him, by the very virtue of his active imagination, remained a prisoner to the myths and fantasies of this world.

I have deepest respect for the pagan myths, still more for the myths in the holy Scriptures.

With this quote above, Lewis seems to reveal his inner quest for truth, which led him from idealism to pantheism and then finally to theism. To taste the mystic flair in his writing, this excerpt from Narnia series might capture our imagination.

Then I fell at his feet and thought, Surely this is the hour of death, for the Lion (who is worthy of all honor) [supposedly the Narnian representation of Christ] will know that I have served Tash [supposedly the Narnian representation of Satan] all my days and not him [the Lion Christ]. But the Glorious One bent down his golden head and said, Son, thou art welcome. But I said, Alas, Lord, I am no son of thine but the servant of Tash. He answered, Child, all the service thou hast done to Tash, I account as service done to me.

When Lewis died at the age of sixty-five, he left the world a rich legacy of forty books. Amongst them, books of fiction, poetry, philosophy, theology and literary criticisms, just to name a few.

C. S. Lewis
A Pilgrim of Christianity

But out of all men's yearning
That She might live, eternally our own
The Spirit's stronghold barred against despair

We know we are not made of mortal stuff
And we can bear all that comes after
For we have seen the Glory, we have seen

She vanishes, and now
The tree grows barer every moment
The leaves fall, a killing air
Sighing from the Country of Men
Has withered it
The tree will die

Fairies must be in the woods
Or the satyr's laughing broods
Tritons in the summer sea
Else how could the dead things be
Half so lovely as they are
How could wealth of star on star
Dusted o'er the frosty night
Fill thy spirit with delight

Atoms dead could never thus
Stir the human heart of us
Unless the beauty that we see
The veil of endless beauty be
Filled full of spirits that have trod
Far hence along the heavenly sod
And seen the bright footprints of God

I cried out for the pain of man
I cried out for my bitter wrath
Against that hopeless life that ran
Forever in a circling path

I saw our planet far and small
Through endless depths on nothing fall
A lonely pin-prick spark of light
Upon the wide, enfolding night

For thou art Lord and hast the keys of hell
Yet I will not bow down to thee nor love thee
For looking in my own heart I can prove thee
And know this frail, bruised thing is above thee
Laugh then and stay, shatter all things of worth
Heap torment on torment for thy mirth
Thou art not Lord while there are men on earth
Who water the flowers and roll the lawn

And sit and sow and talk and smoke
And snore all through the summer dawn
Who sit of evenings by the fire
And are not fretted by desire
Only the strange power
Of unsought Beauty in some casual hour
Can build a bridge of light or sound or form
To lead you out of all this strife and storm

We need no barbarous words nor solemn spells
To raise the unknown, it lies before our feet
There have been men who sank down in Hell
In some suburban street
And some there are that in their daily walks
Have met angels fresh from sight of God
Or watched how in their beans and cabbage-stalk
Long files of faerie trod

Saint Augustine

Lord, grant me chastity, but not as yet.

These are the words of a saint, poet and a mystic, who confessed to God and to the world his countless sins in his own journey to see the Light of Truth.

Augustine was the son of a pagan father, Patricius and a Berber Christian mother, Monica. He had two brothers and one sister. Augustine received his education in classical Latin in a local school. At twelve years of age, he continued his education at Madaura, a center of education in Roman North Africa twenty miles south of Thagaste. His studies were disrupted for one whole year when he was called home due to the lack of funds for his college education. That was when he indulged in dissipation and sexual adventure, recounted in his famous work, *The Confessions*. After a year, he went to study at Carthage, associating with friends called *the wreckers* who hurled him deeper into the abyss of shameful love and dissipation. In Carthage, he met a woman whom he came to love dearly, and she bore him a son, Adeodatus, meaning, God-given. Augustine was only eighteen when his father died, a baptized Christian. Certainly, a seed of hope in the bereavement of his mother, who wanted to hold and behold her family in the folds of Christianity!

Augustine returned To Thagaste to teach rhetoric, but his circle of friends didn't improve, befriending another group known as the, heretical Manicheans. After eight years of teaching, he went to Rome to teach rhetoric, and then to Milan, urged by one of his former student by the name of Alypius. He also began studying the works of Neoplatonists; especially, of Plotinus, who had taught that one is awakened to a sense of divine destiny through purification from carnal appetites. Later, he met a visitor by the name of Ponticianus who told him about St. Anthony and the desert monks of Egypt who had left all they had in the world to devote themselves to the lives of prayer and asceticism.

Augustine began to feel his heart burn in his breast with the power of that call to a life of renunciation was exerting on him. He repaired to the garden of the house, where he wrestled with the demands of his flesh and wept with great, tormented sobs over his inability to accept the challenge of continence. Hearing an unseen child say, 'Take up and read. Take up and read.' Augustine opened the book of St. Paul, which he had been studying, to Romans 13, where he read. 'Let us live honorably as in daylight, not in carousing and drunkenness, not in sexual excess and lust, not in quarreling jealousy. Rather, put on the Lord Jesus Christ and make no provision for the desires of the flesh.' At this moment, confidence and peace flooded into his heart and dispelled the anguish that had overwhelmed him in the garden. Paul's question, 'Who will free me from this body of death?' became Augustine's question. Paul's answer, 'Thanks be to God through Jesus Christ our Lord.' became precisely the truth he long sought. From then on Augustine's life became a journey of quest and suffering to reach the Throne of God. At Milan, Augustine also met the Bishop Ambrose, who became his friend and confidant. During this time, Augustine suffered chest pains and asthma, and retired to Cassiciacum near Lake Como, to rest and recover. He was accompanied by Monica, Adeodatus, Alypius and several other friends, but soon returned to Milan where Alypius and Adeodatus were baptized by Bishop Ambrose. The same year Monica passed away, Augustine returned to Thagaste with his son and friend, establishing a monastic community and living a contemplative life as a *lay servant of God*. Three years later, his son died, and grief-stricken he moved to Hippo with the intention of setting up a monastery. There, he met Bishop Valerius, and for the next eight years wrote extensively against the Donatist heresy, a schismatic group that considered itself the *pure* Church and insisted on rigorously observing ritual actions to the point of fanaticism. One year before the death of Bishop Valerius, Augustine was ordained his assistant, and after his death he himself became the Bishop of Hippo. He remained in this office till his own death, writing his Confessions, and exposing the errors of Arians, Donatists, Pelagians and the Manicheans. *Augustine's Confessions are written as a long prayer addressed directly to God and are an exercise in candor and honesty.*

You have made us for Yourself, and our heart is restless until it rests in You.
St. Augustine

Saint Augustine
The Bishop of Hippo

Creator God, O Lord of all
Who rule the skies, you clothe the day
In radiant color, bid the night
In quietness serve the gracious
Sway of sleep, that weary limbs
Restored to labor's use, may rise again
And jaded minds abate their fret
And mourners find release from pain

O Lord, do I love Thee
Thou didst strike my heart
With Thy word and I loved Thee
But what do I love when I love Thee
Not the beauty of bodies
Nor the loveliness of seasons
Nor the radiance of the light around us
So gladsome to our eyes
Nor the sweet melodies of songs of every kind
Nor the fragrance of flowers ointments and spices

Nor manna and honey
Nor limbs delectable for fleshly embraces
I do not love these things when I love my God
And yet I love a light and a voice and a fragrance
And a food and an embrace when I love my God
Who is a light, a voice, a fragrance, a food
And an embrace to my inner man
This it is that I love when I love my God
Late have I loved Thee
O Beauty so ancient and so new
Too late have I loved Thee
And lo, Thou wert inside me and I outside
And I sought for Thee there
And in all my unsightliness
I flung myself on those beautiful things
Which Thou has made
Thou wert with me and I was not with Thee
Those beauties kept me away from Thee
Though if they had not been in Thee
They would have not been at all
Thou didst call and cry to me
And break down my deafness
Thou didst flash and shine on me
And put my blindness to flight
Thou didst blow fragrance upon me
And I drew breath and now I pant after Thee
I tasted of Thee and now I hunger and thirst for Thee
Thou didst touch me
And I am aflame for Thy peace

I love you, Lord, with no doubtful mind
But with absolute certainty
You pierced my heart with your Word
And I fell in love with you
But the sky and the earth too
And everything in them

All these things around me
Are telling me that I should love you
And since they never cease to proclaim
This to everyone
Those who do not hear me
Are left without excuse
But you, far above, will show mercy to anyone
With whom you have already
Determined to deal mercifully
And will grant pity
To whomsoever you choose
Were this not so
The sky and the earth would be proclaiming
Your praises to the end

O Truth, illumination of my heart
Let not my own darkness speak to me
I slid away to material things, sank into shadow
Yet even there, even from there, I loved you
Away I wandered, yet I remembered you
I heard your voice behind me, calling me back
Yet scarcely I heard it for the tumult of the unquiet
See now, I come back to you
Fevered and panting for your fountain
Let no one bar my way
Let me drink it and draw life from it
Let me not be my own life
Evil was the life I lived for myself
I was death to me, but in you I begin to live again
Speak to me yourself, converse with me
I have believed your scriptures
But those words are full of hidden meaning

Let them turn back and seek you
For you do not forsake your creation
As they have forsaken their creator

Let them only turn back
See! There you are in their hearts
In the heart of all those who confess to you
Who fling themselves into your arms
And weep against your breast
After their difficult journey
While you so easily will wipe away their tears
At this they weep the more
Yet even their laments are matter for joy
Because you, Lord, are not
Some human being of flesh and blood
But the Lord who made them
And now make them anew and comfort them

In a living creature such as this
Everything is wonderful and worthy of praise
But all these things are gifts from my God
I did not endow myself with them
But they are good, and together
They make me what I am
He who made me is good, and he is my good too
Rejoicing, I thank him for all those good gifts
Which made me what I was even as a boy
In this lay my sin
That not in him was I seeking pleasures
Distinctions and truth
But in myself and the rest of his creatures
And so I fell headlong into pains
Errors and confusions
But I give thanks to you, my sweetness
My honor, my confidence to you, my God,
I give thanks for your gifts
Do you preserve them for me
So will you preserve me too
And what you have given me
Will grow and reach perfection

And I will be with you
Because this too is your gift to me
That I exist

Have mercy on me, Lord
And hearken to my longing
For I do not think it arises from this earth
Or concerns itself with gold silver or precious stones
With splendid raiments or honors or positions of power
With the pleasures of the flesh
Or with things we need for the body
And for this our life of pilgrimage
For all those things are provided for those
Who seek your kingdom and your righteousness
Look and see, O my God, whence springs my desire
The unrighteousness have told me titillating tales
But they have nothing to do with your law, O Lord
And see, that law is what stirs my longing
See, Father, have regard to me
And see and bless my longing
And let it be pleasing in your merciful eyes
That I find grace before you
So that the inner meaning of your words
May be opened to me
As I knock at their door

If the tumult of the flesh fell silent for someone
And silent too were the phantasms of earth
Sea and air silent and the heavens
And the very soul silent itself
That it might pass beyond itself
By not thinking of its own being
If dreams and revelations
Known through its imagination were silent
If every tongue, and every sign
And whatever is subject to transience

Were wholly stilled for him
For if anyone listens, all these things will tell him
We did not make ourselves
He made us who abides forever
And having said this they held their peace
For they had pricked the listening ear
To him who made them
And then he alone were to speak
Not through things that are made, but of himself
That we might hear his Word
Not through fleshly tongue nor angel's voice
Nor thundercloud, any riddling parable
Hear him unmediated, whom we love in all these things
Hear him without them, as now we stretch out
And in a flash of thought
Touch the eternal Wisdom who abides above all things
If this could last, and all other visions
So far inferior, be taken away
And this sight alone ravish him who saw it
And engulf him and hide him away
Kept for inward joys
So that this moment of knowledge
This passing moment that left us aching for more
Should there be life eternal
Would not Enter into the joy of your Lord
Be this, and this alone
And when, when will this be
When we all rise again, but not all are changed

O Lord my God, hear my prayer
May your mercy hearken to my longing
A longing on fire not for myself alone
But to serve the brethren I dearly love
You see my heart and know this is true
Let me offer in sacrifice to you
The service of my heart and tongue

But grant me first what I can offer you
For I am needy and poor
But you are rich unto all who call upon you
And you care for us though no care troubles you
Circumcise all that is within me from presumption
And my lips without from falsehood
Let your scriptures be my chaste delight
Let me not be deceived in them
Nor through them deceive others
Hearken, O Lord, have mercy, my Lord and God
O Light of the blind, Strength of the weak
Who yet are Light to those
Who see and Strength to the strong
Hearken to my soul
Hear me as I cry from the depths
For unless your ears be present in our deepest places
Where shall we go, and whither cry
Yours is the day, yours the night
A sign from you sends minutes speeding by
Spare in their fleeting course a space for us
To ponder the hidden wonders of your law
Shut it not against us as we knock
Not in vain you have willed so many pages to be written
Pages deep in shadow, obscure in their secrets
Not in vain do harts and hinds seek shelter in those woods
To hide and venture forth
Roam and browse, lie down and ruminate
Perfect me too, Lord, and reveal those woods to me
Lo, your voice is joy to me
Your voice that rings out above a flood of joys
Give me what I love
For I love indeed, and this love you have given me
Forsake not your gifts, disdain not your parched grass
Let me confess to you all I have found in your books
Let me hear the voice of praise
And drink from you

And contemplate the wonders of your law
From the beginning when you made heaven and earth
To that everlasting reign when we shall be
With you in your holy city

CONCLUSION

The seed of Sufism
Was sown in the time of Adam
Germed in the time of Noah
Budded in the time of Abraham
Began to develop in the time of Moses
Reached maturity in the time of Jesus
Produced pure wine in the time of Muhammad
Shahabudin Suhrawardi

Go, soar with Plato to the empyreal sphere
To the first good, first perfect, and first fair
Or tread the mazy round his followers trod
And quitting sense call imitating God
As Eastern priests in giddy circles run
And turn their beads to imitate the Sun
Go, teach Eternal Wisdom how to rule
And turn into thyself, and be a fool!
Alexander Pope

Oh Sufi, did you know
That 'Brotherhood and Sisterhood'
Is the ship in which we are sailing
On the great waters of
Love, Harmony and Beauty
Guided by the compass
Of the spirit of Guidance
And driven by the energy
Of spiritual liberty
Heading toward the goal
Of the annihilation of ego
Where one may begin
At last to realize
That the sailor is verily

The Divine Presence sailing
In the past, present and future
On the waves of our illusion
Pir Vilayat Khan

BIBLIOGRAPHY

Songs of Kabir translated by Linda Hess and Shukdev Singh

Tales From the Land of the Sufis by Mojdeh Bayat & Mohammad Ali Jamnia

Heart, Self & Soul by Robert Frager

Sufism by Carl W. Ernst

The Circle of Love by Llewellyn-Lee

The Heart of Sufism by Hazrat Inyat Khan

Awakening by Pir Vilayat Inayat Khan

The Journey of the Lord of Power by Ibn Arabi

The Knowing Heart by Kabir Helminski

In the Tavern of Ruin by Javad Nurbakhsh

The Gift (Hafiz) by Daniel Ladinsky

The Rose Garden (Sa'adi) by Edward Rehatsek

Rubaiyat of Omar Khayyam by Edward Fitzgerald

Mystical Poems of Rumi by A. J. Arberry

The Conference of Birds (Attar) by C. S. Nott

Umar Ibn al-Farid by TH. Emil Homerin

Collected Works of C. S. Lewis

Gitanjali by Rabindranath Tagore

The Confessions by Saint Augustine

Glorious Taj and Beloved Immortal by Farzana Moon

ABOUT THE AUTHOR

Farzana Moon is a teacher and a bibliophile. She writes plays, poetry, short stories and historical, biographical accounts of Moghul emperors. Her collection of plays is archived at *Ohio State University*. She has participated in author/panel discussions at Clyde Library and Columbia University. Her published works in the sequels of the Moghuls are: *Babur, the First Moghul in India; The Moghul Exile; Divine Akbar and Holy India; The Moghul Hedonist; Glorious Taj and Beloved Immortal.* Her other published works are: *Holocaust of the East* by Cambridge Scholars Publishing. *Irem of the Crimson Desert* by ATTM Press. *Prophet Muhammad: The First Sufi of Islam* is accepted to be published by the Garnet Publishing UK. *Babur The First Moghul in India: In the Land of Cain; Divine Akbar and Holy India* are reprinted 2nd editions by Hamilton Books. Currently researching for a book about the last Moghul. She is on Facebook.

ALL THINGS THAT MATTER PRESS ™

FOR MORE INFORMATION ON TITLES AVAILABLE FROM
ALL THINGS THAT MATTER PRESS, GO TO
http://allthingsthatmatterpress.com
or contact us at
allthingsthatmatterpress@gmail.com

MAY 23 2015

CPSIA information can be obtained at www.ICGtesting.com
Printed in the USA
LVOW04s1558200415

435320LV00001B/486/P

9 780984 721542